# *Dharma Breeze*

# *Dharma Breeze*

## Essays on Shin Buddhism

**Nobuo Haneda**

Maida Center of Buddhism
Berkeley, California

Maida Center of Buddhism
2609 Regent Street
Berkeley, CA 94704-3314


ISBN 978-0-9790783-0-9

Printed in the United States of America

*Respectfully dedicated to*
*Mr. Yukimasa Tada (1927–2001),*
*the founder of Maida Center of Buddhism*

# Preface

Shin Buddhism and Zen Buddhism are the two major Buddhist traditions in Japan. Although many people in the United States know about Zen Buddhism, not many people know about Shin Buddhism, the teachings of Shinran (1173–1262). Even many of those who call themselves Shin Buddhists are uncertain as to what their religion is all about. Ever since I came to this country from Japan, I have been surprised by Shin Buddhists' different understandings of their religion. Some understand it as an ethno-cultural teaching or an ethical teaching. Some regard it as a mystical teaching. Others interpret it as a religion similar to Christianity that talks about the salvation of the wicked by a loving savior.

One of the basic reasons Shin Buddhism has not been adequately appreciated even by its followers is that its key concepts have not been explained in English in a comprehensive manner. Thus in this book I have attempted to give definitions and explanations of the basic concepts of Shin Buddhism. If my readers find them useful, I will be happy.

This book consists of nineteen essays that I wrote for *The Dharma Breeze*, the newsletter of the Maida Center of Buddhism. I have rather arbitrarily organized them into four divisions. The first division (essays 1 through 4) explains Amida Buddha or the spirit of Dharmakara, the most important basic concept of Shin Buddhism. The second division (essays 5 through 8) deals with the Pure Land and birth in the Pure Land. The third division (essays 9 through 12) deals with "listening," the true practice in Shin Buddhism. The last division (essays 13 through 19) deals with general topics such as the definitions of "Buddhist" and "happiness."

I owe all of the Shin Buddhist ideas expressed in this book to the following five Shin teachers: Rev. Manshi Kiyozawa (1863–1903), Rev. Haya Akegarasu (1877–1954), Rev. Ryōjin Soga (1875–1971), Shūichi Maida (1906–67), and Rev. Rijin Yasuda (1900–81). Rev. Kiyozawa is generally regarded as the most important Shin Buddhist teacher in modern Japan. He reinterpreted Shinran's teachings with modern consciousness and revived the essence of Shinran's spirit. Among his many excellent students, Rev. Akegarasu and Rev. Soga were the two greatest successors to his thought. Then Rev. Akegarasu's spirit was followed by Maida and Rev. Soga's scholarship was followed by Rev. Yasuda. I cannot express my gratitude deeply enough to these five teachers. I only fear that I am misrepresenting their ideas in this book.

Since these essays were written as independent articles in separate issues of a newsletter, they contained redundancies. Although I have attempted to eliminate them in preparing this book, some still remain.

In this book Japanese names are given in Western order, surnames last. All English translations of the original Japanese and classical Chinese texts are mine. In my endnotes I have given their sources and references to other available English translations.

This book is dedicated to Mr. Yukimasa Tada, a student of Shūichi Maida and the founder of the Sun Drug Company in Tokyo. In 1996 I met Mr. Tada in Tokyo for the first time. When he learned that I had been translating and introducing Maida's works in the United States, Mr. Tada offered to help me in my efforts. He founded the Maida Center of Buddhism in Berkeley, California. I am deeply indebted to him.

I am deeply grateful to friends who helped me complete this book. First, I wish to express my sincere gratitude to Mr. Steve Kaufman, my fellow-learner, for reading the manuscript many times and giving me valuable suggestions. I am grateful to Mrs. Diane Ames, whose excellent editorial skill has improved the content of this work, and to Ms. Arlene Kato for making a wonderful cover design and typesetting this book.

I am also grateful to Ms. Jane Ike who initiated the publication of *The Dharma Breeze* newsletter in 1995. She and I came up with the title "Dharma Breeze." In Japan the Buddha-Dharma is often compared to a cool refreshing breeze.

Last, but not least, my sincere thanks to my wife Tomoko. She has been the best Dharma friend and critic for me. So far all my publications have consisted of my translations of texts. This is the first book that consists of my own essays. I feel as if our first baby has been born.

*Nobuo Haneda*
*Berkeley, California*
*September 25, 2006*

# Contents

# General Topics

# Amida Buddha

# 1

# What Is Shin Buddhism?

*The more ripe a cluster of rice becomes,*
*the lower it bows down its head.*

— A Japanese proverb

Shin Buddhism, or the teachings of Shinran (1173–1262), teaches us the importance of humility, the most important universal virtue. Many people think that the ultimate goal in Buddhism as well as human life is to become *good*. But according to Shinran, it is to become *humble*. Being *good* is not good enough; we must become *humble* persons. We must know our evilness, the existence of our ineradicable egoism. We must know our ignorance, the limitations of our intellects. We must become humble persons who can say, "I'm evil and ignorant."

In order to explain that Shin Buddhism teaches us the importance of humility, let me first discuss the two stages of life that Shinran experienced.

## Two Stages in Shinran's Life

The most important event in Shinran's life was his meeting with Hōnen (1133–1212, the founder of the Jōdo [Pure Land] School), when Shinran was twenty-eight. This event divided his life into two stages: the period before the meeting was the first stage and the period after it was the second stage.

When Shinran met Hōnen, Shinran realized that he had had a shallow view of Buddhahood. His thoughts on the subject went through a total transformation. Before Shinran met Hōnen, Shinran thought that a Buddha was a *good* and *wise* person—a holy person who was possessed of wonderful virtues. In order to become such a Buddha, Shinran attempted to purify himself by eliminating evil passions. But he could not attain Buddhahood. Not only was he unable to become a Buddha, he was feeling more and more depressed and miserable. His goal of Buddhahood seemed far away. He could not understand what was wrong.

When Shinran met Hōnen, Shinran saw a Buddha in him. But the Buddhahood that he saw in Hōnen was totally different from what he had anticipated. More than anything else, Shinran was moved by the fact that Hōnen was a humble student. Hōnen identified himself only as a student of Shan-tao (613–81, the fifth Shin patriarch). Hōnen said that the only important thing for him was to learn from his teacher. Thus Hōnen embodied the spirit of a Buddha by the name of *Namu Amida Butsu* (Bowing Amida Buddha). *Namu* (Bowing) is a part of the Buddha's Name. The Buddha's Name symbolizes the humblest human spirit. Before Shinran met Hōnen, he had thought that a Buddha was a teacher, a respected and worshipped person. But now, having met Hōnen, he realized that a Buddha was actually a student, a respecting and worshipping person.

Further, before Shinran met Hōnen, he had thought that a Buddha was a *good* and *wise* person. But now Shinran realized that such an understanding of Buddhahood was a shallow one. He realized that he had been seeing Buddhahood only objectively, from the outside. He had not known the subjective reality of Buddhahood—what a Buddha would say about himself. Although people would see a Buddha from the outside and describe him by saying, "He is good and wise," a Buddha would describe himself by saying, "I'm evil and foolish." Having met Hōnen, who had deep insight into his own evilness and ignorance and said, "I'm evil and foolish," Shinran realized that the true essence of Buddhahood was humility—deep insight into one's own evilness and foolishness.

Thus in the first stage, i.e., before he met Hōnen, Shinran thought that a Buddha was a *good* and *wise* person and made efforts to become such a Buddha. But in the second stage, i.e., after he met Hōnen, Shinran realized that the essence of Buddhahood was humility—studentship and insight into one's own evilness and ignorance.

Thus, having been moved by Hōnen's humble spirit, Shinran also became a humble student. He recognized that he had ineradicable egoism at the basis of his being and that he had no goodness that he could rely on as the basis of his liberation. Thus he stopped all practices designed to transform himself into a holy person. He realized that a wonderful spiritual tradition represented by Hōnen had already been given to him and that the only thing necessary for him was to listen to it. This realization was his liberation.

## Growing and Maturing

Let me further discuss the two stages, calling the first stage "the growing stage" and the second stage "the maturing stage."

Human beings must grow up first; we must learn and experience all kinds of things. We must strive to be good, better, and best; we must pursue infinite possibilities. But when our growing stops, we must enter the maturing stage. We must reflect upon ourselves, know our evilness, ignorance, and ineradicable egoism, and become humble. The growing stage is the stage of self-betterment and self-enhancement; it is a stage of self-affirmation. The maturing stage is the stage of self-reflection and self-understanding; it is a stage of self-negation.

Shin Buddhist teachings concern the maturing stage. Shin Buddhist terms such as "evil" and "ignorant" are all connected with the discovery of our ineradicable egoism, with our becoming humble. Terms such as "evil" and "ignorant" should be understood only within the context of our individual self-understanding. They should be used only within the grammatical context of the first person singular, as in "I'm evil," or "I'm ignorant." The evilness or ignorance of other people is not an important issue in Shin Buddhism.

The essence of Shin Buddhism is the discovery of the evilness, ignorance, and ineradicable egoism in our beings. In the sphere of religion, people usually believe that they deserve liberation or salvation and seek it. But Shin Buddhism teaches us that we, being helplessly egoistic and having no goodness as any basis for

5

liberation, cannot possibly deserve liberation.

Having discovered the ineradicable egoism in his being, Shinran said, "Since I am incapable of performing any religious practice, hell is my only home."[1] He also identified himself as an *icchantika* (one who is totally devoid of any good).[2] However, the discovery of his impossible reality was his liberation. This experience of liberation is a paradox that can be described only with the expression, "No liberation is liberation." When Shinran recognized that he had no goodness that he could rely on as the basis of his liberation, his religious self-reliance was totally shattered. However, this total negation of self-reliance was actually his liberation. Now he became a totally humble person, which was his liberation. In his essay, "The Last Person Remaining,"[3] Rev. Haya Akegarasu (1877–1954, a Shin teacher) described this paradoxical experience of liberation: "Our liberation does not exist in our becoming liberatable and liberated; it exists in our knowing that we are totally unliberatable."

In his essay, "Self-Despising and Self-Respecting,"[4] Rev. Manshi Kiyozawa (1863–1903, a Shin teacher) described the liberation of the humble person by saying:

> The person who has entered the gate of religion sees "zero" value in himself. Far from slighting or respecting the self, he does not recognize any value in the self. Both our anguish and grief exist because of our sense of self-importance. If we have already lost our sense of self-importance, we do not feel anguish and grief. If we have already lost it, we do not mind whether others despise or honor us, or whether they slight or respect us. We can do all things calmly, leaving others to respect or despise us as they like.

Once a Buddhist Sunday school teacher asked me, "Can children comprehend Shinran's deep self-awareness?" I answered, "No, I don't think children can fully comprehend Shinran's deep self-awareness, because it belongs to the maturing stage. Children are still in the growing stage."

Growing must come first. We must let children grow up first. It is only after they finish growing up that they start to mature. When they enter the maturing stage, they can understand what Shinran says about himself. It is exactly the same with academic education. No matter how important graduate education may be, we cannot skip grammar school and junior high school. Thus Shinran called the growing stage the "Necessary Gate (*yō-mon*)."[5] It is a preparatory stage. It is only after we go through the growing stage that the maturing stage can begin.

Another Buddhist Sunday school teacher asked me, "Is it all right for children to have ambition? Should we Sunday school teachers encourage or discourage children's ambition?" I answered, "There is nothing wrong with children having ambition. It is important that they have ambition."

Let children have as much ambition as possible. Let them pursue whatever goals or ideals they have. Let them strive to become great scholars, scientists, artists, and sportsmen. If, after having pursued their ambition and become adults, children start to reflect upon themselves and see their limitations, then their maturing stage has begun. While they are attempting to realize their ambitions, their arrogance will grow, too. But if they start to recognize their own arrogance, then their maturing stage has begun. Let them grow up first. Let them grow up as big as possible. We should not make *bonsai* trees—miniature Shinran trees—out of children. In a photo such a *bonsai* tree may look like a huge Shinran tree. But it is not the real Shinran. Shinran was a gigantic tree. In his growing-up stage, Shinran grew up to be a huge tree. If a ten-year old boy says, "I'm evil and ignorant," there is something wrong with him. If Sunday school teachers are attempting to make children say that, they are creating monsters.

Then what can Sunday school teachers do for children? The only thing they can do is to prepare children for the maturing stage in their future. The teachers must tell them that becoming good is not good enough—that the ultimate goal in human life is to become humble. They must tell them that humility is the most important universal virtue and that only a humble person can have the greatest happiness and joy.

More than anything else, Buddhist Sunday school teachers themselves must learn to be humble; they must learn to gain insight into the pettiness of their being and have deep respect for the Dharma ("truth" or "teaching"). If Sunday school teachers simply attempt to teach ideas and concepts to children, they fail to be good teachers. But if they can manifest humility, deep respect for the Dharma, they are good teachers. Children will eventually forget most of the ideas and concepts that their teachers have taught them, but they will remember the humble attitude and respect that they have seen in their teachers.

## An American Girl and Paderewski

There is a story about an American teenage girl who was sightseeing in Germany. One day she visited Beethoven's house. When she saw the piano that was used by Beethoven, she, being an accomplished pianist, could not resist her desire to play it. Thus she sat on a chair in front of the piano and played one of her favorite numbers. Since she played well, some tourists in the room clapped their hands. She was proud of herself.

After playing, she moved from the chair and started to look at the things, such as lamps and books, which were used by Beethoven. Then an elderly gentleman came into the same room. When he came to Beethoven's piano, he sat on the chair where the girl had played music a little while before. The elderly gentleman sat there quietly. He looked as if he were meditating.

The girl was curiously watching him. Then a tourist approached her and whispered into her ear, "Do you know who that gentleman is? He is Paderewski, a famous Polish pianist. He is probably the greatest pianist alive today."

She had heard much about Paderewski, but she had never seen him before. She was very excited to see such a famous pianist before her eyes. She thought that Paderewski would play music on the piano just as she had done a little while before. She waited and waited, but he did not start playing. Minutes passed. But he did not play.

The girl became impatient. She finally approached Paderewski and said, "Mr. Paderewski, aren't you going to play?" The master answered, "No." She said, "Mr. Paderewski, it would be a great honor for us if you would let us listen to your music." Paderewski answered, "No, Miss, I am sorry. I won't play now. As a matter of fact, I cannot play. I cannot play music on this piano. This is the piano of Beethoven, my teacher. Miss, I am nothing before this piano, before my teacher. I am totally worthless. I am not worthy even to touch this piano." When she listened to his words, she was deeply moved.

Let me comment on this story. The two pianists in this story, the American girl and Paderewski, show us two different stages in human life—the growing stage and the maturing stage. The girl represents the growing stage and Paderewski the maturing stage. Both were excellent pianists. But there was a considerable difference between them. The girl was a *good* pianist—a capable and skillful pianist; but Paderewski was a *humble* pianist, a great pianist.

The difference was that Paderewski had deeper respect for Beethoven than the girl did. The girl certainly had some respect for Beethoven; but her respect could not be compared with Paderewski's. He had tremendous respect for the great composer. He knew his limitations, smallness, and worthlessness before him. He was nothing before him. He was completely bowing down his head before him.

It is one thing to be *good*. But it is quite another to be *humble*. Being *good* is not good enough. We must know the limitations, smallness, and emptiness of our being. A *good* person must become a *humble* person. The girl must become a Paderewski.

Besides deep understanding of the pettiness of our being, besides humility, besides deep respect for the Dharma, what else do we need in our lives? If we are truly bowing our heads before the Dharma, that is itself our liberation. Shinran's view of liberation is fully expressed in his words at the end of his "Verses of True Entrusting (*Shōshin-ge*)," "Just entrust yourself to the words of these [seven] great monks."[6] He says that if we can *truly* respect and bow our heads before our teachers, that is all there is to Buddhism; nothing else is necessary. Our liberation is fully realized there.

Many people think that Buddhism means a practice or efforts to perfect themselves. But the most important thing in Buddhism is not practices or efforts to perfect ourselves; it is the realization that something perfect—a wonderful Dharma tradition—is already given to us. We need only to receive it, to listen to it.

The most important thing in Buddhism is not *whatness*—not what we can do or achieve. It is *howness*—how humbly we are respecting the Dharma and how deeply we are bowing our heads before it. Our lives' focus must shift from *whatness* to *howness*, from becoming a good person to becoming an evil person—a humble person.

# 2

# What Is Hongan?

"Hongan" is a term that is familiar to Shin Buddhists. But being familiar does not mean that we have an accurate understanding of it. It is often the case that we have a shallow, if not wrong, understanding of it. Since a good understanding of this term is crucial to understanding Shin Buddhism, let me discuss it.

The Japanese term "Hongan" consists of two words, "*hon*" and "*gan*." The meanings of these two words are as follows:

> *Hon* (Skt. *purva*): "basic," "original," "primal," "former," and "ancient"
>
> *Gan* (Skt. *pranidhana*): "desire" and "vow"

"Hongan" has two basic meanings: (1) "Basic Desire," the literal meaning; (2) "Original Vow." In the first meaning, which is broad and general, "Hongan" means a "desire" to become a Buddha. In the second meaning, which is narrow and specific, it means a "vow" that a bodhisattva makes to become a Buddha. Although these two meanings, "desire" and "vow," are connected, they refer to two different aspects (or stages) in Buddhist experience: (1) when one meets a Buddha, he awakens a "desire" to become a Buddha; (2) when the desire becomes very strong, he makes a "vow" (or "resolution") to become a Buddha.

I consider it unfortunate that most English translators of Shin texts have translated "[Hon]gan" only as "[Original] Vow." When "[Hon]gan" is translated only as "[Original] Vow," it sounds like a concept that belongs only to some specific individuals; it is difficult to see the universal implication that is contained in the concept. It is true that in some places in Shin texts we must translate "[Hon]gan" as "[Original] Vow." But translating it as "[Original] Vow" all the time contributes to the mystification of Shin teachings.

However, when we translate "[Hon]gan" as "[Basic] Desire," we can easily see its universal implication. What, then, is the "Basic Desire"? It is the most basic and fundamental human desire, the oldest and earliest human desire. It is the desire that differentiates human beings from other animals. It is the aspiration to be a Buddha (a real human being)—to live the most meaningful and fulfilling life as a human being. It is extremely important to know that "Hongan" in the sense of "Basic Desire" does not belong to some specific individuals; it belongs to all human beings.

Let me discuss "Basic Desire" within the context of the life of Shakyamuni, the founder of Buddhism.

Tradition says that when Shakyamuni was young, he did not know the reality of human suffering. But when he grew up, he left the palace and witnessed the reality of human suffering in the form of old age, sickness, and death. He became extremely depressed. Then one day Shakyamuni went out of the palace again and met a traveling monk whose face was brilliantly shining. Shakyamuni was deeply impressed by him. Having discovered an ideal human being in the traveling monk, he could not suppress his desire to become a person like him. It was because of this desire that he left his palace to seek Buddhahood.

I believe that Shakyamuni's encounter with a traveling monk was the most crucial event in his life. Meeting a person of "Basic Desire," Shakyamuni's "Basic Desire" was awakened. An aspiration to become a Buddha was awakened in him. It was because of this "Basic Desire" that he sought Buddhahood and eventually attained it.

Let me explain how the concept of "Amida" came into being. After the passing of Shakyamuni, Buddhism gradually became a highly monastic and academic tradition: the initial spirit of Shakyamuni was lost. Early Buddhists (the so-called Hinayana followers) had tremendous respect for Shakyamuni's teachings. And partly because of this respect for their teacher, they turned Shakyamuni's teachings into a fixed system of thought. They were mainly concerned with memorizing, preserving, and transmitting it. They treated his teachings as if they were "finished products."

But about three centuries after the passing of Shakyamuni, there appeared a movement called the Mahayana that challenged the Hinayana. Mahayana followers criticized Hinayana followers for creating a fixed system of thought. They were not satisfied with merely knowing Shakyamuni's teachings as "finished products"; they wanted to know the creative source of inspiration that produced Shakyamuni, i.e., the universal basis of his spirit. To use an expression by Rev. Ryōjin Soga (1875–1971, a Shin scholar), they wanted to know not only the spiritual essence of Shakyamuni but also that of "the Buddhism before Shakyamuni."[7] They identified the universal basis of his spirit as "Basic Desire (Hongan)" and came up with the concept of "Amida" (or "Dharmakara") as a symbol for it.

To explain this universal basis of Shakyamuni's spirit, Mahayana followers composed texts such as the *Larger Sukhavativyuha-sutra* (henceforth the *Larger Sutra*). The *Larger Sutra* talks about how Dharmakara ("Storehouse of the Dharma"), an ideal seeker, becomes a Buddha by the name of "Amida." When Dharmakara meets his teacher, he is deeply impressed by him and awakens a "desire" to become a Buddha like his teacher. Then he makes "vows" to become a Buddha and engages in a passionate practice called "eternal practice." He eventually fulfills his "desire" (or "vows") and becomes a Buddha by the name of Amida.

The essential message of the text is that "Dharmakara" symbolizes the "Basic Desire" or "Innermost Aspiration." Rev. Ryōjin Soga identifies "Dharmakara" with "latent consciousness (*alaya-vijnana*)" that is deeply hidden in all human hearts.[8] When we meet a person who embodies "Dharmakara" (or "Basic Desire"), we are deeply moved by him and experience liberation.

"Amida" (or "Dharmakara") is not a god or divine savior. He is a symbol for the "Basic Desire" in the human heart. Although the meaning of Amida is such, Amida has often been mistaken for a divine savior like the Christian God. Although Buddhism does not talk about anything divine, mysterious, or superhuman, Amida has often been mistaken for a divine savior.

This misunderstanding of Amida is prevalent not only in the United States but also in Japan. In modern Japan, some Shin teachers attempted to rectify this misunderstanding of "Amida." Rev. Haya Akegarasu was one of those Shin teachers. After many years of struggle he reached what he considered the true meaning of Amida. Earlier in life, Akegarasu believed that Amida was a divine savior like the Christian God. But when he experienced a spiritual crisis at age thirty-seven, his view of Amida went through a total transformation.

Akegarasu was born in a Shin Buddhist temple and was exposed to the traditional Shin doctrines that were systematized during the Edo period (1600–1867). According to him, traditional Shin doctrines made him view Amida as a divine savior who existed outside himself. Akegarasu believed that he was a totally helpless sinner; that Amida, therefore, made a vow to save him out of compassion; and that when he put his faith in Amida, Amida saved him.

An important event that contributed to Akegarasu's later reinterpretation of Amida took place when he was a high school student. It was his meeting with his teacher, the Rev. Manshi Kiyozawa. Kiyozawa challenged Akegarasu's traditional view of Amida. Kiyozawa wanted Akegarasu to be awakened to the deeper meaning of Amida. But while Kiyozawa was alive, Akegarasu's view of Amida did not change.

But in 1913, when Akegarasu was thirty-seven, his wife passed away; in the following years some tragic events took place. These years are called the period of Akegarasu's crisis. In this period Akegarasu thought about quitting the ministry, emigrating to a foreign country, or even committing suicide.[9]

It was then that Akegarasu's Amida as a divine savior crumbled. His faith in the grace of Amida crumbled as well. He finally realized that it was a mistake to understand Amida as an external divine savior. In one of his works, Akegarasu talks about his spiritual crisis and the subsequent demise of the Amida in whom he had believed:

> Once I believed that the Power Beyond the Self [*ta-riki*] meant the Buddha's power, and that we were going to be saved by the external power of Amida Buddha. But when my soul experienced a deep crisis, the Buddha who was standing before me disappeared and I became helpless, unable to rely on anything.[10]

In this way Akegarasu's faith in Amida collapsed. He could not find anything that he could depend on. He faced absolute emptiness. This was the time when he even thought about suicide. But in this agony, he heard a shout that came from the innermost part of his being. He realized that the deepest reality in his being was this shout. He says:

> Then, out of my desperate desire that something be done there appeared the self. A Buddha did not appear. People did not appear. The self shouted powerfully, "O, myself! O, myself!" The self did not shout, "O, God!" The self shouted, "O, myself!" Its voice told me, "Don't shout 'O, God!' Don't shout 'O, Buddha!' Live your true life and shout, 'O, myself!'"[11]

Akegarasu's deepest shout was not "O, Buddha!" It was "O, myself!" It was a shout gushing out of his life itself. He says that this shout was the voice of Amida. He realized that Amida was actually his own "Basic Desire." It was by discovering Amida within himself, by feeling its power within himself, that he could experience liberation. This, he says, is the true meaning of what Shinran teaches as "liberation through the Power of the Basic Desire (or Innermost Aspiration)."

If we asked Rev. Akegarasu, "What is Amida for you?," I believe that he would answer that Amida took two forms in his life: first, Amida took the form of his teacher Kiyozawa—an external voice that challenged Akegarasu; second, it took the form of the "Basic Desire"—Akegarasu's own inner voice that gushed out of himself. In order to further explain these two forms that Amida takes, let me give a simple illustration here.

Suppose a chick is sound asleep inside an eggshell. Outside the eggshell there is a mother chicken. In an attempt to awaken the chick, she is desperately pecking the shell from outside and shouting, "Awaken, my baby! Come out, my baby!" Although she is pecking and shouting hard, the chick's sleep is so deep that he does not know that she is shouting. But since her voice gets louder and louder, he gradually realizes that a voice is coming from outside the shell. Finally he clearly recognizes her voice, which awakens his desire for birth. Now he hears a voice from within himself, a voice saying, "Be born!" Being moved by the power of the internal voice, he starts to peck the shell from within. Through the cooperation of the mother and the chick, the shell gets broken and the chick is born.

Now we can talk about the two forms that Amida takes, i.e., Amida's external voice and its internal voice.

First, Amida's external voice is like the calling voice of the mother chicken that comes from outside the shell and urges the chick to be born. What, then, is Amida's external voice in more specific terms? It is the voices of *our Buddhist teachers*. For Shakyamuni, it was the voice of the traveling mendicant. For Akegarasu, it was the voice of Rev. Kiyozawa. There is nothing mysterious or superhuman about this calling voice from outside. It is the voices of our *human* teachers, of the individuals who exist in historical contexts. It refers to their words and teachings.

Second, Amida's internal voice is like the calling voice that comes from within the chick and urges him to seek birth. Just as the mother's external voice awakens the chick's desire from within himself, our teachers' voices awaken the "Basic Desire" from within us.

The first (external) voice is absolutely necessary for the second (internal) voice—the "Basic Desire"—to arise. Because our "Basic Desire" is so deeply hidden within ourselves and we are not even aware of possessing it, we cannot awaken it by ourselves. We must have it awakened by the first voice, by our teachers.

Although the first voice is absolutely indispensable for our birth or liberation, we must know that it cannot be our ultimate refuge. The first voice is like a midwife who assists at our birth. Its role is to guide us to the second voice. The most important thing, the thing that eventually realizes our liberation, is the second voice—our own "Basic Desire" that is awakened within ourselves.

I would like to conclude this essay with a famous statement that is attributed to the Buddha. According to tradition, when the Buddha was born, he took seven steps and declared, "Above the heavens and below the heavens, I alone am most noble." This statement succinctly summarizes the essence of Buddhism.

When Shakyamuni Buddha said "above the heavens and below the heavens" he was talking about the two types of gods in whom the people of his time believed. When he said "above the heavens" he was talking about heavenly gods. When he said "below the heavens" he was talking about earthly gods. Saying, "Above the heavens and below the heavens," he was indicating that he does not need any gods, any external divine saviors. When he said, "I alone am most noble," he was talking about the "Basic Desire" in his being. He said that his "Basic Desire" was most noble. This is the tradition of Shakyamuni Buddha and Shinran. This is the tradition of "liberation through the power of the Basic Desire."

# 3

# What Is Amida Buddha?

The concept of "Amida" (i.e., a Japanese form of the two Sanskrit names of a Buddha: *Amitabha* [Limitless Light] and *Amitayus* [Limitless Life]) is probably the most important concept in Shin Buddhism. But people often have a shallow understanding of it. Or, worse, they often misunderstand it. If we have a wrong understanding of the concept of "Amida," our understanding of Shin Buddhism is totally wrong.

In this essay I will discuss three topics. First, I will discuss the historical background of the appearance of "Amida" in India. Second, I will define "Amida." Third, I will explain the meanings contained in Amida's Name, *Namu Amida Butsu*.

## Historical Background of the Appearance of "Amida" in India

Here I will first discuss the contents of Shakyamuni Buddha's enlightenment and then explain how the concept of "Amida" appeared in India approximately three centuries after Shakyamuni's death.

Tradition tells us that when Shakyamuni was born as a prince in a small kingdom in India, he was given the name Siddhartha. Siddhartha grew up without knowing the reality of human suffering. But when he became a young man, he went out of the three gates of the palace and saw the reality of human suffering, of old age, sickness, and death. He learned that those things were inevitable and that all the things he had cherished must be lost some day. He became extremely depressed. Then one day, he went out of the fourth gate and met a traveling monk. The monk's face was shining because of his wisdom. Having met this awakened person, Siddhartha awakened his aspiration to become a Buddha. When he was twenty-nine, he left his family to seek the way.

After Siddhartha left his family, he visited spiritual leaders of his time. Although he studied various doctrines and practices under them, he thought that they could not lead him to the ultimate peace he was seeking. Thus he renounced them and sat under a tree. With firm determination, he told himself, "Never shall I stir from this seat until I have attained the most perfect enlightenment." He started to meditate.

His meditation under the tree eventually led him to enlightenment. In his meditation, Siddhartha asked, "What am I? Do I have something permanent in myself?" He examined his body, things such as his skin, muscles, bones, and blood. He also examined his mind, things such as sensation, conception, volition, and consciousness. Then, he realized that everything in his body and mind was constantly moving, changing, and flowing and that there was nothing permanent.

One morning, when Siddhartha looked at the morning star, he attained enlightenment. He understood that there was nothing permanent outside himself or inside himself. When he clearly understood the Dharma, i.e., the truth of impermanence, he became a Buddha, an Awakened One. Insight into the Dharma was the content of his enlightenment.

Although we usually say that Shakyamuni attained the Dharma, it is more accurate to say that Shakyamuni "was attained by the Dharma," an expression by the Zen master Dōgen (1200–53, the founder of the Japanese Sōtō Zen School).[12] The Dharma's killing and reviving Shakyamuni are called his enlightenment.

When Shakyamuni experienced enlightenment, he said, "My life is already spent. The Holy Work is already established." These two sentences describe the two—negative and positive—aspects of the Dharma and of his enlightenment experience. Since these two aspects are quite important, let me elaborate.

The negative aspect of the Dharma (i.e., the truth of impermanence) initially appeared to Shakyamuni as a negative force (taking the form of old age, sickness, or death). This negative force destroyed all his ideas, thoughts, and opinions. It did not allow him to be attached to anything. The total negation of the self (or spiritual death) that he experienced in encountering the negative force is described in his words, "My life is already spent." This was a very humbling experience. We can say that he became a humble person.

When he experienced total negation of the self, the Dharma turned into a positive force. The Dharma initially appeared to him as a negative force because he was seeing it from an attached perspective. But now that he had lost his attached perspective, he no longer saw the Dharma as a negative force. He now saw the Dharma as a positive force, as a dynamic and creative force. He realized that all existing things were constantly new, fresh, and lively. He realized that they were the creative elements of the creative world and that he himself was one creative element in the creative world.

The fact that he became one with the Dharma, the dynamic and creative force, means that he started to live his life as a constant seeker and learner, as an appreciator of his ever-fresh ordinary life. This is expressed in his words: "The Holy Work is already established." We can say that he became a dynamic (or creative) person.

Hence, having been attained, i.e., killed and revived, by the Dharma, he became a "humble and dynamic" person. The humility and dynamism that were realized in him by the Dharma were two sides of the same coin. Only a truly humble person can engage in dynamic seeking activities.

The core of Buddhism is *how* Shakyamuni lived, not his ideas and teachings. Buddhism spread, and many people took refuge in it, mainly because they were moved by Shakyamuni's "humble and dynamic spirit" and desired to emulate it. But after his passing it was often the case that his vital spirit was forgotten and only his ideas and teachings were honored and studied.

Not long after Shakyamuni's death in the fourth century B.C., the Buddhist tradition called the Hinayana appeared in India. The Hinayana developed as follows. When Shakyamuni died, his disciples lost their beloved and revered teacher. They regarded Shakyamuni as the founder of a new religion. Since they thought that he had left a perfect and definitive teaching, they considered it their mission to faithfully memorize his teachings and preserve them. They did so because they had deep respect for their teacher. Having deep respect for the teacher is an admirable thing. But at the same time, there is often a danger involved in it. Out of their respect for their teacher, they started to categorize, systematize, and academicize his teachings. They started to dogmatize them. During the first few centuries after Shakyamuni's death, his teachings came to be fixed, formalized, and, to use a stronger expression, fossilized. This tradition is called the Hinayana.

It was in this historical context that the Mahayana, another major Buddhist tradition, appeared in India around the first century B.C., approximately three hundred years after Shakyamuni's death. The Mahayana appeared as a reaction against and criticism of the Hinayana, as a revivalist movement. In the eyes of Mahayanists, Hinayanists were attached to lifeless ideas and concepts. Mahayanists believed that the most important thing in Buddhism was not the ideas and concepts, i.e., the finished products that were produced by Shakyamuni, but his creative spirit itself. In the eyes of Mahayanists, Hinayanists were seeing only the footprints of a rabbit; they were not seeing the dynamic and lively life of the rabbit itself. Hinayanists were interested in that which Shakyamuni produced, not in the source of inspiration that produced Shakyamuni.

Mahayanists were interested in identifying the universal source (or basis) of the inspiration that awakened and produced Shakyamuni.[13] And they identified it as the Dharma or universal Buddhahood. In order to show this spiritual basis of Shakyamuni in a more concrete human form, Mahayanists created the concept of "Amida"—an ideal human being, a "humble and dynamic" human being who embodies the Dharma.

Mahayanists described this ideal human being in Mahayana texts such as the *Larger Sutra*. The earliest version of this *sutra* was composed in India in approximately the first century B.C. The *Larger Sutra* tells the story of a seeker by the name of Dharmakara. Dharmakara symbolizes the "Innermost Aspiration" or "Basic

Desire." The "Innermost Aspiration" means the primordial human aspiration—an aspiration that makes humans humans. It means an aspiration for Buddhahood that is entertained by all human beings. After performing many difficult practices, Dharmakara fulfills his "Innermost Aspiration" and becomes Amida Buddha.

The *Larger Sutra* was translated into Chinese and became one of the most popular *sutra*s in Sino-Japanese Buddhism. The Pure Land tradition that is based on the *sutra* became one of the major Buddhist traditions in China and Japan. Shinran considered the *Larger Sutra* the most important textual basis of his Buddhism. Now I have discussed the historical background of the appearance of "Amida" in India. With this historical background in mind, let us define "Amida."

### The Definition of "Amida"

Amida is "a personal symbol." In other words, Amida is "a fictional character" like Hamlet or Faust. Let me explain this definition by first discussing what Amida is not. Since "Amida" is a fictional character, he is (1) *not* a god (or a divine being) and (2) *not* a historical person.

First, Amida is *not* a god. Just as Hamlet symbolizes certain spiritual qualities of human beings and does not have any superhuman (or divine) meaning, "Amida" symbolizes certain spiritual qualities of human beings and does not have any superhuman (or divine) meaning.

Second, Amida is *not* a historical person. Just as Hamlet is a fictional character created by Shakespeare and not a historical person, Amida is a fictional character created by ancient Indians and is not a historical person. Hamlet is supposed to be a prince of Denmark, but we cannot find his name in the actual chronicle of Denmark. Similarly, there is no actual history of "Amida"; being a symbolic (fictional) figure, Amida never lived in any specific time and place.

Next, let us discuss what "Amida" is, what he symbolizes. We can say that "Amida" symbolizes two things: (1) Shakyamuni, a historical person, and (2) the Dharma (ultimate reality or truth) or universal Buddhahood.

First, "Amida" symbolizes Shakyamuni, a historical person. Just as Strickland, the hero of Summerset Maugham's novel *The Moon and Sixpence*, is a symbol of the painter Gauguin, a historical person, "Amida" can be considered a symbol of Shakyamuni, a historical person. We can say that "Amida" symbolizes the "humble and dynamic spirit" of Shakyamuni. As we have seen, Mahayanists created the concept of "Amida" in order to criticize the fossilized doctrines of Hinayanists and restore the vital spirit of Shakyamuni.

Second, "Amida" symbolizes the Dharma or universal Buddhahood. Mahayanists created the concept not only to express the vital spirit of Shakyamuni, but also to show the spiritual basis of Shakyamuni and all human beings. They wanted to show that just as Shakyamuni was awakened and liberated by the Dharma or universal Buddhahood, all human beings are awakened and liberated by it.

Thus, as far as our personal attainment of Buddhahood is concerned, this second meaning of "Amida" as a symbol of the Dharma or universal Buddhahood is more important than the first. The goal in Buddhism is that we personally become Amida Buddhas.[14] The Buddhahood that we are expected to attain in Buddhism is not the historical Buddhahood of Shakyamuni, but the universal Buddhahood that is symbolized in "Amida." We cannot totally identify with Shakyamuni, because we live in a different historical context than that of Shakyamuni. However, we can and should identify with the universal aspiration that Dharmakara symbolizes, strive to fulfill it, and become Amida Buddhas. We must realize our deepest reality, our true selves, which is what the realization of Amida Buddhahood means.

Here I want to pose a question concerning the doctrinal relationship between Shakyamuni and the Mahayana. What would Shakyamuni say about the Mahayana? Would he say, "Mahayanists, you have distorted my teachings and deviated from them"? I believe that Shakyamuni would endorse the Mahayana, because he emphasized the importance of the Dharma and universal Buddhahood as the basis of his enlightenment.

Shakyamuni never claimed to have created the Dharma. He identified himself as a person who was awakened and liberated by the Dharma. The discovery of the Dharma that had existed before him was called enlightenment. He emphasized the importance of relying upon the Dharma, saying, "Rely upon the Dharma; don't rely upon a human being."[15] Shakyamuni taught them that they should not look at Shakyamuni, a physical existence that perishes, but at the Dharma that does not perish.

The same thing can be said about Buddhahood. Shakyamuni taught that the Buddhahood that had existed before him awakened and liberated him. Thus it is not right to say that Shakyamuni was the first Buddha. In some early Buddhist texts, Shakyamuni said, "There were seven Buddhas in the past." As we have noted earlier, when Siddhartha went out of the fourth gate of the palace, he met an awakened person, a Buddha. It was because of this meeting that an aspiration for Buddhahood was awakened in him. Thus, Buddhahood existed before Shakyamuni, and it awakened his aspiration for Buddhahood.

Because Shakyamuni taught that the Dharma and Buddhahood that had existed before him were the most important basis of his enlightenment experience, we can say that Mahayanists' emphasis on the importance of "Amida" is in total agreement with what Shakyamuni taught. Now let us examine the meanings contained in Amida's Name.

## Meanings Contained in Amida's Name, *Namu Amida Butsu*

In Shin Buddhism, Amida's Name, "*Namu Amida Butsu* (i.e., the six-character Name)," is the most important thing. The reason it is considered the most important thing in Shin Buddhism is that it is one of the most compact and excellent expressions of the essence of Buddhism. *Namu Amida Butsu* means "Bowing Amida Buddha."[16] This Name expresses the "humble and dynamic spirit," the essence of Buddhahood.

Now in order to understand the meanings contained in the Name, we must examine the story of Dharmakara in the *Larger Sutra*. At the beginning of the story, Dharmakara meets his teacher and expresses his joy by praising his teacher. After receiving instructions from his teacher, Dharmakara makes his vows and engages in a practice called "eternal practice." And he eventually becomes a Buddha by the name of "Bowing Amida Buddha."

Here it is important to know the contents of his practice, because his practice crystallizes into his Name. Although he takes up various practices, such as precept keeping and meditation, the most important practice Dharmakara performs is *kuyō* (which is the Japanese term for the Sanskrit term *puja*). Because of this *kuyō* practice, Dharmakara becomes a Buddha by the name of "Bowing Amida Buddha."

Although *kuyō* is usually translated as "making offerings to a Buddha," it implies the whole process of learning. It implies that a student visits his teacher, worships and praises him, gives offerings to him, serves him, and studies under him. Thus, *kuyō* basically means that a student visits a teacher and studies under him.

The *Larger Sutra* emphasizes the importance of *kuyō* practice in many places. For example, in the "Verses in Praise of a Buddha (*Sambutsu-ge*)" Dharmakara says, "Even though there are zillions of Buddhas and great sages as many as the sand grains of the River Ganges, I will visit all of them and study under them (i.e., *kuyō*)"[17]; and in the "Verses of Repeated Vows (*Jūsei-ge*)" he says, "I will visit all the Buddhas and study under them (i.e., *kuyō*), thereby acquiring roots of virtue."[18]

*Kuyō* is a practice in which Dharmakara perfects his "humble and dynamic studentship," being gradually emptied (killed) and permeated (revived) by the Dharma. The humbler he becomes, the more Buddhas he discovers and worships. The more Buddhas he discovers and worships, the humbler he becomes. Dharmakara gradually loses his attachment to himself—to his own ideas and opinions. He sees less importance in himself. At the same time, he deepens his respect for Buddhas, for his teachers, and intensifies his practice of *kuyō*. The speed with which he studies the Dharma accelerates.

The nature of Dharmakara's *kuyō* practice becomes clear when we refer to the *Essentials of the Eight Schools* (*Hasshū-kōyō*), a traditional Japanese Buddhist textbook composed in the thirteenth century. It says that a bodhisattva goes through forty stages of *kuyō* practice and reaches the forty-first stage of Buddhahood. The forty stages of *kuyō* practice are divided into the following four divisions: (1) the first thirty stages (i.e., from the first to the thirtieth), in which a bodhisattva worships Buddhas as many as the sand grains of five Ganges Rivers; (2) the six stages (i.e., from the thirty-first to the thirty-sixth) in which he worships Buddhas as many as the sand grains of six Ganges Rivers; (3) the three stages (i.e., from the thirty-seventh to the thirty-ninth) in which he worships Buddhas as many as the sand grains of seven Ganges Rivers; (4) the fortieth stage, in which he worships Buddhas as many as the sand grains of eight Ganges Rivers.[19]

This text shows that a bodhisattva intensifies his practice of *kuyō* at an accelerated pace. The closer he gets to Buddhahood, the more Buddhas he worships. In this way, the text teaches us that the perfection of Buddhahood is the perfection of *kuyō* practice.

The text, however, does not say anything about the number of Buddhas the Buddha in the forty-first stage of Buddhahood worships. Does this mean that the Buddha in the forty-first stage does not worship Buddhas? No, on the contrary, it means that the Buddha in the forty-first stage can worship a limitless number of Buddhas. When a bodhisattva becomes a Buddha, his entire being becomes the practice of *kuyō* itself. He now sees all human beings as Buddhas and worships them. For a Buddha, not only all animate things but also all inanimate things are Buddhas. Since his entire life is *kuyō* practice, he is not even aware that he is doing *kuyō*.

Because of *kuyō* practice Dharmakara has become a Buddha by the name of "Bowing Amida Buddha"—a Buddha who bows his head before all existing things, considering them Buddhas. "Bowing Amida Buddha" means that Dharmakara has become a Buddha because of his "Bowing." "Bowing" and *kuyō* practice are synonymous.

"Bowing (*Namu*)" is the most important part of the Name. Thus we can say that the most important thing in Buddhism is not *whatness* (i.e., things such as ideas, concepts, and theories) but *howness* (i.e., "bowing"). In Buddhism we are not moved by a person of *whatness* but by a person of *howness*. A person of extensive scholarship and knowledge may impress us, but cannot shake us from the bottom of our hearts. We are moved by a person who is humbly and dynamically seeking—a person who is permeated by the truth of impermanence. I believe this is the manner in which Buddhism has been transmitted to us. If Buddhism were only *whatness*, it would have perished a long time ago. Buddhism has survived and has been transmitted to us because there have been many individuals who embodied the "humble and dynamic spirit."

Shin Buddhism is a religion of *howness*, of "bowing." It is not a religion of assertion or propagation. In Shin Buddhism, meeting a person who embodies "Bowing Amida Buddha" is very important. The person of "Bowing Amida Buddha" does not have any intention of teaching or converting other people. When we meet such a person, we cannot help being shaken by him. When we meet a "Bowing Amida Buddha," his "Bowing" speaks to us in a silent and quiet, yet powerful, way. His "Bowing" tells us, "You should bow your head, too!" Thus in his "Interpretation of the Six-Character Name" Shinran says, "'Bowing (*Namu*)' means an absolute command in which the Innermost Aspiration calls us to come."[20]

Thus the "Bowing" in the Buddha's Name has two aspects: the first is that Dharmakara has become a Buddha because of his "Bowing" (or *kuyō*); the second is that Dharmakara's "Bowing" exerts spiritual influence upon others, becoming a silent calling voice. The first is called the self-benefiting (or "going") aspect; the second is called the others-benefiting (or "returning") aspect. Here it is extremely important to know that these two aspects are two sides of the same coin; they are contained in Dharmakara's single practice of "bowing." The only thing Dharmakara did was to perfect his own "bowing." It is a mistake to think that Dharmakara took two different actions—that he *first* took self-benefiting action and *then* took an others-benefiting action.

Only when we meet a bowing person can we bow our heads.

When Shinran met Hōnen, he saw a "Bowing Amida Buddha" in him. Shinran was shaken by Hōnen's humble and dynamic spirit. And Shinran also came to embody "Bowing Amida Buddha." That was Shinran's liberation. Having been permeated by the spirit of Dharmakara, Shinran lived the life of a humble and dynamic seeker. Throughout his life he identified himself only as a student of Hōnen. He never claimed that he was a teacher. In the *Tannishō* (A Record in Lament of Divergences) he says, "I, Shinran, do not have even one single disciple."[21]

When I was twenty-two, I met a Buddhist teacher by the name of Shūichi Maida (1906–67). He embodied the spirit of Dharmakara—the spirit of *kuyō* practice. He kept on learning from many teachers, many Buddhas. I was deeply moved by his humble and dynamic spirit. Although I was studying Russian at that time, I became interested in Buddhism. Since then I have been studying Buddhism.

We do not have to talk about many things in Buddhism. Only one thing—becoming a true student—is good enough. If we can realize it in our lives, that is our liberation. Everything important in Buddhism is contained in it. Becoming a true student is the highest goal, the ultimate goal, in Buddhism. If we are hoping to attain something more dramatic than that, we are just dreaming a Buddhist dream. We are liberated, not by an external being or force, but by *the bowing that is realized in us.*

## Conclusion

In order to restore the universal basis of Buddhahood, the "humble and dynamic spirit," Mahayanists created the symbol of Amida (or Dharmakara). Amida symbolizes a human spirit that keeps on advancing without being complacent with whatever it has attained. But unfortunately, the Mahayana that challenged the stagnation and fossilization of the Hinayana also became stagnant and fossilized when it became the predominant Buddhist tradition in India in the centuries following. Then later, in the Sino-Japanese Buddhist tradition, there developed new Mahayana traditions, such as the

Pure Land tradition, that challenged and criticized earlier Mahayana traditions that had become stagnant and lifeless. Individuals like Hōnen and Shinran criticized the fossilized Mahayana tradition. They attempted to revive the fresh and creative spirit of Buddhism.

Hōnen and Shinran were humble students, but this does not mean that they were passive; they were the greatest rebels of their times. They were not satisfied with lifeless Buddhist doctrines. They challenged those complacent Buddhists whose teachings were fossilized. Since the two masters became a threat and danger to such people, they were persecuted by them.

But unfortunately the tradition of Hōnen and Shinran also became stagnant and fossilized when it became one of the major Buddhist traditions in Japan. Shinran's vital, creative spirit was totally forgotten immediately after his death. Shinran's successors, led by his descendants, created a sectarian dogma, a rigid and fossilized dogma. They created a doctrine in which Amida is presented as if he were a divine savior. The true meaning of Amida as a symbol with which all human beings should identify was totally forgotten.

Thus in modern Japan, Shin Buddhist teachers such as Rev. Manshi Kiyozawa, Rev. Haya Akegarasu, and Rev. Ryōjin Soga had to reinterpret "Amida" in their modern consciousnesses and revive its original meanings. Amida is a symbol of the "humble and dynamic spirit." In our personal lives we must meet a person who embodies this spirit and discover "Amida" in ourselves. When we personally become one with it and become humble and dynamic students, we experience liberation.

# 4

# Liberation by
# Limitless Light (Wisdom)

## Introduction

Among various symbols used in Shin Buddhism, "light" that symbolizes "wisdom" is probably the most important. The original Sanskrit word for Amida, who is the liberator-Buddha in Shin Buddhism, is *amitabha* (limitless light). *Amitabha* (limitless light) is the symbol of limitless wisdom.

Buddhism is a religion of wisdom. It is not a teaching of being saved by gods, or by external powers. In Buddhism, the power of wisdom that our teachers awaken in us liberates us. The power of wisdom is put into a personal symbol: Amida. Amida is not a savior like the Christian God, who is believed to be an actual being. Although Amida is presented in Buddhist literature as if he were an actual human being, he is not an actual human being; he is a literary device to show us the importance of the power of wisdom. Thus, strictly speaking, it is not right to say that there is an actual being (or savior) called Amida and that he has wisdom. The limitless wisdom that has the power of liberating us is real and is symbolically called Amida. I want to discuss here in this essay what it means to be liberated by Amida (limitless light).

## Rennyo's Five Conditions for Spiritual Liberation

First, I want to discuss the importance of the symbolism of light by discussing the "Five Conditions for Spiritual Liberation (*gojū no gi*)"[22] that Rennyo (1415–99, a Shin Buddhist teacher) taught. This schema shows the important role light plays in our experience of spiritual liberation. The five conditions are as follows:

1. A good karmic background
2. A teacher
3. Light (wisdom), i.e., Amida (limitless light)
4. Awakening (*shin*)
5. The Name (which means "saying the Name of the Buddha [i.e., *Namu Amida Butsu*]")

First, Rennyo talks about the importance of having a good karmic background, such as receiving a human existence and being born in a good spiritual climate. Second, he emphasizes the importance of meeting a teacher, a historical individual who transmits the Dharma to us.

It is because of meeting with a teacher that we can meet light (wisdom), the third condition. Although a teacher is quite important, it does not mean that the teacher's personal qualities are important. It is the light that is coming through him that is important. The teacher has received it from his teacher and is transmitting it to us.

Fourth, as a result of our meeting a teacher and light, we experience the awakening that is the most important part of this schema. Fifth, the Name (which means "saying the Name of the Buddha") means a concrete manifestation (or expression) of our awakening experience. Rennyo indicates here that deep spiritual awakening cannot help manifesting itself in our lifestyle.

## A Passage in the *Larger Sutra*

In order to see these five conditions for spiritual liberation in a more concrete context, let me discuss one passage in the *Larger Sutra*, the basic text of Shin Buddhism.

This passage is found near the end. In the preceding sections, Shakyamuni Buddha has given Ananda, the main recipient of teaching in the *sutra*, a discourse about how Amida Buddha realized his Buddhahood and created his land, and how people can be born in that land. Having listened to Shakyamuni's teaching, Ananda now experiences awakening (*shin*), a crucial spiritual transformation. This passage describes his awakening experience.

Let me quote the passage:

> The Buddha said to Ananda, "Stand up! Rearrange your robes, put your palms together, demonstrate your sincere reverence, and worship Amida Buddha! ..."
>
> Ananda stood up and rearranged his robes. Keeping the right posture and facing the west, he demonstrated his sincere reverence. He put his palms together, prostrated himself on the ground, and worshipped Amida Buddha. Then Ananda said to Shakyamuni, "World-Honored One, please let me see Amida Buddha, his land of peace and happiness, and the great assembly of bodhisattvas and *sravaka*s (disciples)."
>
> As soon as Ananda had said this, Amida Buddha emitted a great light that universally illuminated all the Buddha-lands... It was like seeing the flood at the end of a period of cosmic change that fills the whole world; all existing things are totally immersed in it... The light of Amida Buddha was precisely like that flood. All the lights of *sravaka*s and bodhisattvas were outshone, and only the Buddha's light kept on shining bright and glorious.
>
> At that time Ananda saw that the brilliance of Amida Buddha's dignity was so great that it was like Mt. Sumeru, that rises above all kinds of worlds. There was no place that was not illuminated by the light emanating from Amida Buddha.[23]

Here we can see three of the five conditions for spiritual liberation: a teacher, light (wisdom), and awakening (*shin*). A teacher refers to Shakyamuni Buddha. It was through listening to Shakyamuni's teachings that Ananda was able to see light (wisdom). And Ananda experienced awakening and liberation.

Having recognized that Ananda has deepened his desire to see Amida Buddha, Shakyamuni tells him, "Stand up! Rearrange your robes." Then, for the first time in his life Ananda sees Amida Buddha, limitless light. This passage says that Amida's light illuminated all the Buddha-lands. Light is compared to a flood and Ananda is totally immersed in it.

## Human Wisdom and Amida's Wisdom

Now we have discussed a passage that describes the crucial spiritual transformation of Ananda. Having faced Amida, limitless light (wisdom), for the first time in his life, Ananda realizes that the light (wisdom) he has so far cherished is totally overshadowed by Amida's limitless light. The passage says, "All the lights of *sravaka*s and bodhisattvas were outshone, and only the Buddha's light kept on shining bright and glorious." This means that the wisdom of Ananda, who is a *sravaka* (disciple), is totally overwhelmed by Amida's wisdom.

Here two forms of wisdom are contrasted, human wisdom and Amida Buddha's wisdom. Now let me discuss what they are.

What is the regular human wisdom that Ananda cherished before his encounter with limitless wisdom? What is the regular wisdom that we also cherish in our daily life? It is dualistic wisdom (or the dualistic way of thinking), which Shinran calls *ji-riki* (self-power). It is the wisdom in which we divide things into two. We talk about life and death, good and evil, right and wrong, purity and impurity, and happiness and unhappiness. We love positive values (like life, goodness, and happiness) and try to ignore negative values (like death, evil, and unhappiness). We build our lives on the basis of positive values and wish that negative things not exist in our lives.

Here one important point has to be noted. Although many Buddhist teachers criticize human wisdom, the dualistic way of thinking, as something erroneous and to be eliminated, it is not the dualistic way of thinking itself that is erroneous. It is our *attachment* to the dualistic way of thinking and our *overestimation* of it that are erroneous and cause various problems in our lives. Our dualistic way of thinking is so basic and indispensable in our lives that I do not think we can eliminate it. Thus Buddhism teaches us that our *attachment* to it must be eliminated, not the dualistic way of thinking itself.

In the sphere of religion, too, people talk about dualistic ideas, such as "heaven and hell," "enlightenment and delusion," "nirvana and samsara," and "the Pure Land and the impure land." They desire to attain positive values and eliminate negative values by praying to superhuman powers (such as gods and buddhas), or by disciplining themselves or by practicing meditation.

But if we are attached only to positive values and do not see any meaning in negative values, then only half of our life has meaning. Only things such as life, goodness, beauty, and happiness have meaning; the opposite negative values do not have any meaning whatsoever. If we live our lives that way, our lives will end up in total meaninglessness, because the end of our lives will be negative—our death and the loss of all the things we cherish.

What, then, is the limitless wisdom of Amida Buddha? Limitless wisdom means *the spirit that limitlessly keeps on seeking and discovering new meaning in all things one experiences in this life.* It means the spirit that is not satisfied with fixed meanings, or with loving only positive values and hating negative values.

In the *Larger Sutra* Dharmakara symbolizes the initial (or causal) stage in which aspiration for limitless wisdom is awakened; and Amida (whom Dharmakara becomes) symbolizes the fruit (or effectual) stage of the realization of limitless wisdom. Before Dharmakara makes his vows and takes up his practice to realize Buddhahood, he describes how he will realize his limitless wisdom in the "Verses in Praise of a Buddha":

> Even though there are zillions of Buddhas
> And great sages as many as the sand grains of the River
>    Ganges,
> I will visit all of them and study under them.
> Nothing is greater than seeking the way, continuously
>    advancing and never retreating.
>
> Even though the Buddha countries are as innumerable
>    as the sand grains of the River Ganges,
> And other lands are also without number,
> My light will illuminate all those countries and lands,
>    spreading all over them.
> Such will be the way I will make continuous efforts, and my
>    power will be limitless.[24]

35

These two verses show the essence of Dharmakara's spirit. Here he says that he will keep on learning from innumerable Buddhas and will deepen and expand his wisdom, and he will eventually have limitless wisdom. With this limitless wisdom, he says that he will embrace all things that he encounters in his life. He will discover new meaning in all things that exist in this world. His wisdom is called the "wisdom that transforms the negative into the positive." He is determined to discover new meaning in all things that are usually rejected as meaningless by human wisdom.

After saying these words in the "Verses in Praise of a Buddha," Dharmakara makes his so-called Forty-eight Vows; then, he performs practices, fulfills his vows, and becomes a Buddha by the name of Amitabha—limitless light (wisdom).

Being attached to the positive values in our dualistic way of thinking, we see only superficial meaning in all things in our lives. However, all things we encounter in our lives have deeper and undiscovered meaning in them. That meaning is waiting to be discovered.

Dharmakara (or Amida) is a symbol of the human spirit that humbly and dynamically keeps on discovering new meaning in all things one experiences. When we meet an authentic teacher in our lives, we see in him a Dharmakara, a humble and dynamic spirit. Then, our attachment to dualistic values is challenged and we are transformed into humble and dynamic seekers; we start to seek new meaning in all things.

Now I have discussed what limitless wisdom means. It means the spirit of a perpetual seeker who desires to discover new meaning in all things. Dharmakara (or Amida) means an all-encompassing spirit—the ocean-like spirit that desires to encompass all.

The passage that talked about the experience of Ananda said that Ananda was totally immersed in the flood of Amida's limitless light. It means that Ananda's dualistic wisdom was totally overshadowed and replaced with the all-encompassing wisdom of the Buddha. It means that the entirety of Ananda's life started to shine. Not only positive things in his life but also what he had considered negative and meaningless in his life started to shine and have meaning. Now, having been totally embraced by limitless light, Ananda had nothing in his life that he should throw away as meaningless. Since this internal transformation took place, we call Ananda's encounter with limitless light his experience of awakening and liberation.

## Rev. Ōmori's First Flower Arrangement

Here let me give you a couple of examples of what limitless wisdom means. Let me first talk about one experience Rev. Shinobu Ōmori (1914–87, a Shin teacher) had.

One day Rev. Ōmori attended a class in flower arrangement for the first time in his life. When Rev. Ōmori sat in the art class, the master of flower arrangement gave him the materials (branches and flowers) for making a flower arrangement. Having received those materials, Rev. Ōmori tried to make his first flower arrangement, selecting good branches and flowers. But he had a hard time finding good materials. After having thrown some useless materials into a trash can, he picked up a couple of branches and flowers and somehow made his first flower arrangement. When all the students finished making their art works, the teacher came to examine them.

When the teacher came to him, Rev. Ōmori told the teacher, "Teacher, I somehow made this arrangement. Sorry, I could not find good materials." Then the teacher put his hand into the trash can and picked up from it some materials that Rev. Ōmori had thrown away. Then, the teacher immediately made a beautiful flower arrangement using those very branches and flowers. Rev. Ōmori was amazed to see the wonderful flower arrangement made by the teacher.

In commenting on this episode, Rev. Ōmori said:

> I threw away those branches and flowers because I thought them totally useless. But the teacher found usefulness in them and made a beautiful piece of work using them. This shows the difference between a foolish person and a wise person. A foolish person considers some things useful and meaningful, and other things useless and meaningless; and

37

he throws away useless things. But a wise person finds usefulness and meaning in everything, even in those things that a foolish person considers useless. A wise person knows that all things are useful and meaningful. *It is not that materials have fixed usefulness, value, or meaning in them. It is our mind, our wisdom, that determines whether a thing has usefulness, value, or meaning.* A foolish person is attached to his fixed value system and discriminates. He says, "This is good, that is bad, this is right, that is wrong, this is useful, that is useless." But a wise person does not have such a fixed value system; with the flexible mind of a humble student, he keeps on discovering new usefulness, new value, new meaning in all things he encounters in his life. A wise person can discover new value and meaning in the things that a foolish person considers meaningless.

Here Rev. Ōmori is saying that the master of flower arrangement had Dharmakara's wisdom (i.e., the wisdom of transforming the negative into the positive). Just like Dharmakara, who saw limitless meaning in all things, the master saw limitless beauty and usefulness in all branches and flowers.

## Waste Material and Earthworms

Let me give you another story. I read this story in a book written by Dr. Iwao Hosokawa (1919–96, a Shin teacher who was a professor of chemistry).

In one pulp plant they had a lot of industrial waste. After making paper using the pulp and extracting useful chemicals from it, they had a tremendous amount of waste material left. Although many people spent a lot of time trying to figure out a way to make use of the waste, they could not find a way to do so. The waste was totally inorganic and useless.

But finally a man came up with a brilliant idea to turn what seemed totally useless into something useful. He turned the waste material into very good fertilizer. This is what he did. He put tons of earthworms into the waste. Then, the earthworms started to eat it. When worms ate the waste, they digested it and excreted it. This way, after several months the worms digested the entire mass of waste and turned it into castings, fine organic fertilizer.

In this story we can see a good example of the power of Dharma-kara's wisdom (i.e., the wisdom of transforming the negative into the positive). The transforming power of worms is a good example of the power of Amida's wisdom.

What seemed totally useless was turned into something quite useful by the power of earthworms. Likewise, in our lives what seems a totally meaningless human experience is turned into a very meaningful human experience by Amida's wisdom.

When living worms go into the dead and inorganic waste, they turn it into living organic material. Likewise, when truly living power (Amida's spirit) goes into a lifeless world, it transforms the lifeless world into a living world.

When light comes into a dust-filled room, even the dust starts to shine. Likewise, when the power of Amida's wisdom enters our lives, all the things that have seemed totally meaningless in our lives, such as our mistakes, failure, sickness, accidents, frustration, struggle, and agony all start to have new meaning.

## Conclusion

It is so important that we meet a teacher and receive light, the wisdom of transformation, from him. It is so important that we receive wisdom, the spirit that keeps on seeking new meaning in life. Hōnen received wisdom from his teacher Shan-tao. Shinran received it from Hōnen. All our predecessors received it from their respective teachers. The more wisdom we receive from our teachers, the deeper the appreciation we have for everything we experience in our lives.

In Buddhism there are many terms that describe human liberation, such as "enlightenment," "attainment of Buddhahood (or nirvana)," "birth in the Pure Land," and "*shinjin* (awakening [realized through listening])." Although many people give all kinds of definitions of human liberation in explaining those terms, I believe that the essence of what is expressed in them must be just this: meeting a teacher and receiving limitless wisdom (the wisdom of transformation). It must mean just receiving a humble and dynamic spirit that limitlessly keeps on discovering new meaning in all things we experience in our lives. I cannot think of the concrete meaning of human liberation in any other way.

# The Pure Land

# 5

# What Is the Pure Land?

## Introduction

The Japanese word for Shin Buddhism is *Jōdo Shinshū* ("True School of the Pure Land"). *Jōdo* means "Pure Land." The unique feature of Shin Buddhism is that it talks about the concept of "the Pure Land" as one of the most important things. Thus without a good grasp of this concept, we cannot understand Shin Buddhism.

However, among all Shin Buddhist concepts, the Pure Land seems to me the most difficult to understand. Traditionally, on a folklore level, many people believed in the literal descriptions of the Pure Land in the *sutra*s (that talk about wonderful things to be enjoyed there, such as delicious foods, wonderful music, and the comfortable climate) and desired to enjoy them in the Pure Land after their deaths. But this literal interpretation of the Pure Land—an interpretation based on affirmation of human greed and attachment—goes against Buddhism which challenges these things. Thus the Pure Land masters cautioned people not to take descriptions of the Pure Land literally. For example, T'an-luan (476–542, the third Shin patriarch) said, "If people hear that they will constantly experience pleasure in the Pure Land and desire to be born there because of that, they will not be born there."[25]

We must know that just as Buddhas (like Amida and Vairocana) and bodhisattvas (like Maitreya and Manjushri) are symbols, places such as the Pure Land and hell are also symbols. What, then, does the Pure Land symbolize? Buddhist scholars often explain that the Pure Land is a symbol for the ultimate truth, nirvana, or suchness. But their explanations often complicate, rather than clarify, the issue. Thus in this essay, I will attempt to present what I consider a simple and concrete interpretation of the Pure Land—an interpretation given by Rev. Rijin Yasuda (1900–82, a Shin teacher).[26] I will attempt to answer the following four questions: (1) "What does the Pure Land symbolize?"; (2) "Why did Dharmakara (or Amida Buddha) create the Pure Land?"; (3) "What is the power of the Pure Land?"; and (4) "Who can be born in the Pure Land?"

## What Does the Pure Land Symbolize?

Before I answer this question, let me first discuss how the *Larger Sutra* depicts the Pure Land. According to the *sutra,* the Pure Land consists of three components: (1) Amida Buddha, the master of the land; (2) innumerable bodhisattvas, the people in the land; and (3) the things in the land, such as the ground, trees, rivers, lakes, and houses. Let me talk about these respectively.

The first component of the Pure Land, Amida Buddha, is the master of the land. The Pure Land is a place where Amida Buddha is teaching and his spirit pervades. Who, then, is Amida Buddha? What is his spirit? Amida Buddha is a symbol of the perpetual seeker and his spirit is the spirit of the perpetual seeker.

The *Larger Sutra* says that Amida was originally a seeker by the name of Dharmakara. When Dharmakara met his teacher, he awakened his aspiration to become a Buddha and create a wonderful Buddha-land. Dharmakara then asked his teacher for instructions on the creation of the Buddha-land. Using the example of a person emptying the ocean and finally obtaining a treasure that lies at its bottom, the teacher told Dharmakara that if he kept on seeking a treasure (i.e., Buddhahood), he would eventually be able to attain it. This instruction became Dharmakara's spiritual basis.

What, then, does it mean to "seek a treasure (i.e., Buddhahood)" in Buddhism? When we are first told to "seek a treasure," we generally think that there is a qualitative difference between "seeking" (the process) and "treasure" (the goal). We think of it just as we think of drilling for oil, in which drilling is the process and oil is the goal. But if we think so, we are misunderstanding the teaching about "seeking a treasure." In Buddhism there is no qualitative difference between the process and the goal; there is no "treasure" (or goal) apart from "seeking" (the process). The "treasure" (or goal) means perfect seeking, the perfect process. Process is "seeking" and the goal is "perfect seeking." Thus, "seeking a treasure" means that we seek perfect seeking or perfect seeker-hood.

The reason I say so is that the only Dharma (truth) that Buddhism teaches us is the truth of impermanence. The truth of impermanence is the freshness of life, or creativeness of life. When this truth starts to permeate us and we start to embody this truth, we become seekers; we can no longer be complacent with fixed values. Then, what do we seek? We seek to fully seek—to fully embody the truth. We seek to become a perfect seeker—one who fully embodies the truth.

The *Larger Sutra* says that Dharmakara attained the "treasure" and became a Buddha. This means that Dharmakara fully embodied the truth of impermanence—that he became a perfect seeker and learner. Thus when Dharmakara became a Buddha, he became a Buddha by the name of *Namu Amida Butsu* (Bowing Amida Buddha). His Name means that he has become a Buddha who is constantly "bowing his head before all Buddhas"—that he is constantly showing respect for them and learning from them. His Name means the fulfillment of the deepest human aspiration—the aspiration to live a rich, full, and creative life. His spirit of perfect studentship pervades every corner of the Pure Land.

The second component of the Pure Land is the bodhisattvas (seekers), the people in the land. In the Pure Land there are innumerable bodhisattvas. They have come to the Pure Land from all the ten directions, because they wanted to emulate the spirit of Amida. In the Pure Land, Amida is constantly teaching the Dharma to them; and they are passionately and diligently listening to him.

The third component of the Pure Land is the things in the land, such as the ground, trees, rivers, lakes, and houses. Whenever things in the Pure Land make sounds, those sounds turn into the sounds of the Dharma. For example, whenever the ripples of rivers or the leaves of trees generate sounds, their sounds become the sounds of the Dharma. In this way, all things in the Pure Land are constantly teaching the Dharma to the people in the land.

To summarize, the essence of the three components of the Pure Land is the same; it is the Dharma, the truth of impermanence. Amida Buddha is a perfect seeker, an embodiment of the truth of impermanence, and his spirit of perfect studentship pervades everywhere; all people in the land are diligently learning to have his spirit; and everything in the land is teaching the Dharma.

What, then, does the Pure Land symbolize? When I read the above depiction of the Pure Land in the *Larger Sutra*, the term that immediately comes to my mind is "the Sangha"—a place where a teacher and his students are wholeheartedly seeking the Dharma. I believe that the Pure Land is a symbol of "the Sangha." This is probably the most concrete way of defining the Pure Land.

In this connection, I recollect the following words of Rev. Rijin Yasuda that he uttered in one of his lectures:

> People say various things about birth in the Pure Land. But could there be any greater "birth in the Pure Land" than the fact that we are now sitting and learning the Dharma to- gether? ... *This place where we are listening to the Dharma together is the Pure Land.* Our being allowed to be part of this place, of this Sangha, is "birth in the Pure Land."
>
> Do you think that you can have anything greater than this in your life—the fact that you are listening to the Dharma as a member of the Sangha? Some people may speak about the wonderful things to be obtained in the Pure Land after death, but those things are nothing but projections of hu- man greed. The fact that we are privileged to be part of the Sangha is our liberation, our "birth in the Pure Land."[27]

Now I have said that the Pure Land is a symbol of the Sangha—a place where a teacher and his students are wholeheartedly seeking the Dharma. In short, it is a place where we can have true friends.

This definition of the Pure Land as the Sangha—as a place where we can have true friends, is consistent with the definition of the Pure Land by Shan-tao. Shan-tao defines this shore and the other shore (i.e., the Pure Land) in his famous parable of "The Two Rivers and White Path." He defines this shore: "The wilderness where no human being is seen. One constantly follows evil friends, without ever meeting a true teacher."[28] He defines the other shore (i.e., the Pure Land): "The traveler immediately reaches the western shore; he meets his good friend(s), and his joy is limitless."[29] Shan-tao explains that this shore symbolizes the world of loneliness or solitude where one does not have any true friend; the other shore (i.e., the Pure Land) symbolizes the world where one has true friends.

Thus, Buddhism simply confirms the importance of the truth that all of us already know—the truth that friends are important in our lives. The place where we can have true friends (the Sangha) is symbolized as "the Pure Land." Entering such a place is called birth in the Pure Land. Having true friends is the greatest happiness and liberation taught in Buddhism. Buddhism does not talk about any greater happiness or liberation.

## Why Did Dharmakara (or Amida) Create the Pure Land?

As far as Dharmakara's aspiration for Buddhahood is concerned, he was no different from other bodhisattvas, because all bodhisattvas aspire to become Buddhas. But Dharmakara was different from other bodhisattvas in that he aspired to create the Pure Land, a Buddha-land. Then why did he create the Pure Land? It was because he was concerned with the liberation of the inferior—those who cannot easily attain liberation because of their heavy karmic evil, and he needed a Buddha-land *specifically* for them.

The *Larger Sutra* says that Dharmakara meditated for five *kalpas*—an inconceivably long time—to formulate his plan for creating a Buddha-land that is designed for the liberation of the inferior. If Dharmakara had been concerned only with the liberation of the religiously superior, he need not have meditated such a long time. An analogy is this. It does not take a long time to discover cures for diseases like stomachaches; but it takes a long time to discover cures for diseases like AIDS. Likewise, Dharmakara had to meditate a long time in order to discover a cure for the incurable—in order to create a Buddha-land that is *specifically* designed for the liberation of the inferior.

Why, then, was it necessary for Dharmakara to create a Buddha-land for the liberation of the inferior? This question, I believe, is an extremely important question for those who wish to understand the basic features of Shin Buddhism. Let me answer this question with the following story.

Once upon a time there was a teenage boy named John in a country town in the state of Montana. From an early age, he wanted to become a dancer. He initially thought that he could become a professional dancer all by himself. Thus, having bought many books on dancing, he started to learn dance steps from them. But, since he was not very talented, it was not easy for him to reach his goal.

One day John met his uncle, whom he deeply respected. Having known that John was interested in dancing, his uncle told him, "John, there is a wonderful dance school named the Astaire Dance School in Hollywood. Please trust my words and go to Hollywood and enter the school. There are no requirements for admission. Just trust my words and enter it. If you enter the school, you'll be surprised by the rapid progress you'll make."

Since John was a trusting boy, he trusted his uncle's words. He went to Hollywood and entered the Astaire Dance School. When he entered the school, he was deeply impressed by it. The teacher and his students there had a tremendous passion for the art; they were all burning with the desire to perfect it. As soon as John entered the school, the passionate atmosphere there immediately influenced him. He could not help practicing dancing for hours and hours every day. Thus, although he was not exceptionally talented, he made rapid progress and became one of the best dancers in the school. And eventually he became a famous dancer; his name was known all over the country. He later started his own dance school and many young people came to study there.

I have created this story with the life of Shinran in mind. The Shin Buddhist implications of the story are as follows: John is Shinran; his uncle is Hōnen (Shinran's teacher); the dance school is the Pure

Land; entrance into the school is "birth in the Pure Land"; making rapid progress is attaining "the stage of non-retrogression,"[30] and becoming an accomplished dancer is "becoming a Buddha."

This story shows that the school (i.e., the Pure Land) was important and indispensable for an ordinary person like John (i.e., Shinran), who did not have exceptional talent and could not reach his goal all by himself. Without entering the school (i.e., being born in the Pure Land) John could not find a way to become an accomplished dancer (i.e., a Buddha). It was not John's abilities that realized his goal. It was the powerful and contagious atmosphere of the school, the power of the burning aspiration entertained by the teacher and students (i.e., Amida and the bodhisattvas) of the school, that totally transformed John. Thus, for an ordinary person like John, entrance into the school was quite important and necessary.

The chief doctrinal feature of Shin Buddhism is that it talks about the Pure Land. Amida, a symbol of limitless compassion, considered that those who are inferior needed a place where they could become Buddhas. Thus he created the Pure Land specifically for them.

The Pure Land is a symbol of the Sangha. Birth in the Pure Land is a symbol of becoming part of the Sangha—a living Buddhist tradition that consists of great teachers. For those who consider themselves religiously superior, the Pure Land (the Sangha) may not be necessary. But for those who recognize the limitations of their abilities, the Pure Land has extremely important meaning. It is absolutely necessary. It is entirely due to the power they receive in the Pure Land that they are transformed into Buddhas.

### What Is the Power of the Pure Land?

Here I want to discuss the specific meaning of the power of the Pure Land that transforms us. When I talk about the power of the Pure Land (or Amida Buddha) that transforms us, some people may think that I am talking about some mysterious power. But Buddhism is not a form of mysticism; there are no mysterious elements whatsoever in Buddhism. The power of the Pure Land means the power of the words of historical teachers, human teachers.

Shin Buddhism teaches us the importance of the words that we hear from our predecessors. It teaches us that *listening to their words alone* brings about our birth in the Pure Land and eventually our Buddhahood. In order to explain the Shin Buddhist emphasis on the exclusive importance of listening, let me talk about the process of making smoked salmon.

To make smoked salmon, we must first put salmon into a smoke box. Then, we must keep them in the box for several days. During that time those salmon will be exposed to the smoke. After several days, we take them out of the box and find that they have become smoked salmon.

The Buddhist implications of this example are as follows: salmon symbolizes us human beings; a smoke box symbolizes the Pure Land (the Sangha); entrance into a smoke box symbolizes birth in the Pure Land (the Sangha); and becoming perfectly smoked salmon symbolizes becoming Buddhas.

If salmon are put into a smoke box and kept there for a certain length of time, they will never fail to become full-fledged smoked salmon. It is not the talents or abilities of salmon that transform them into smoked salmon; it is the power of the smoke that transforms them into full-fledged smoked salmon.

Here two things are important: "smoke" and "exposure to the smoke." In human life, the "smoke" means "words"; and "exposure to the smoke" means "listening to words." Just as exposure to the smoke alone creates smoked salmon, *listening to the words alone* realizes Buddhahood.

As far as Shinran was concerned, his birth in the Pure Land meant not only that he became part of a specific historical fellowship that formed around Hōnen, but also that he became part of the great Buddhist tradition of the seven patriarchs to which Hōnen guided him. For Shinran the seven patriarchs were all Buddhas, i.e., historical appearances of Amida Buddha. It was through listening to their words alone that Shinran was able to become a Buddha. Thus, Shinran emphasized the exclusive importance of listening to their words. For example, at the end of his *"Verses of True Entrusting,"* he says, "Just entrust yourself to the words of these [seven] great monks."[31] Here Shinran indicates that "entrusting (*shin* or *shinjin*)" means "listening." According to him, there was a tremendous joy in listening and listening alone realized Buddhahood.

The Pure Land (the Sangha) is a place where a living Buddhist tradition is maintained—a place where we are exposed to the words of our teachers and are transformed into Buddhas. This spiritual transformation through listening is technically called "listening-perfuming (Skt. *sruti-vasana*)." Although all Buddhist schools emphasize the importance of listening, Shin Buddhism is unique in teaching that *listening alone* is necessary.

## Who Can Be Born in the Pure Land?

Now let me discuss the last question, "Who can be born in the Pure Land?" I have earlier noted that Amida Buddha created the Pure Land specifically for the inferior—those who cannot attain liberation because of their heavy karmic evil. This means that only those who know the limitations of their abilities—who know themselves to be evil and ignorant—can be born in the Pure Land. Those who have moral or intellectual pride cannot be born there.

In other words, the only thing necessary for birth in the Pure Land is "bowing (*namu*)." Otherwise, one cannot be born in the Pure Land. To illustrate the importance of "bowing," let me tell a story about Hideyoshi (1536–98, a samurai ruler of Japan) and Rikyū (1522–91, the systematizer of the art of the tea ceremony).

When Hideyoshi became the ruler of Japan, he summoned Rikyū, a famous tea master, to serve him as his tea maker. Rikyū is known as the original designer of the tea house. The tea house that Rikyū designed was a small cottage-like house, consisting of only two *tatami* mats. A tea master makes tea inside the house; and guests enter it through a tiny entrance. The design of the entrance is unique; it is located at the bottom of a wall. Thus when guests enter the house, they have to stoop to fit into the small entrance at the bottom of the wall. It looks as if the guests are bowing their heads before the tea master who sits inside the house.

Rikyū had deep insight into Buddhism. He knew that in order to enter a noble realm, one had to bow his head deeply. Rikyū knew that unless one became a bowing person, a humble person, he could not enter such a realm. He knew that "bowing" was the only requirement for entrance.

Thus the only thing that was necessary for Hideyoshi, the samurai general, to enter the tea house was to bow—to enter it through the lowered entrance. He had to take off his samurai sword, which meant that he had to forget all about his power, fame, prestige, and pride. He had to become a naked human being, a humble and ignorant human being.

But Hideyoshi could not bow. He thought Rikyū was an arrogant teacher, demanding complete submission from the ruler of Japan. He thought that Rikyū demanded that the ruler of Japan bow his head before him. He thought that he could not take such a humiliating action before one of his subjects. Thus eventually, because of the antagonism and frustration that Hideyoshi felt toward Rikyū, he ordered Rikyū to commit *harakiri*. Having received the order, Rikyū committed *harakiri* and died. In order to enter the tea room the only thing necessary was "bowing." But Hideyoshi could not do that.

The Pure Land is precisely like Rikyū's tea house. It is the spiritual realm of *Namu Amida Butsu* (Bowing Amida Buddha). It is a land permeated with the "bowing (*namu*)" spirit—a student's spirit. In order to be born there (to be part of the Sangha), the only thing necessary is "bowing"—to become humble students.

## Conclusion

The Pure Land is a symbol of the Sangha—a place where people are seriously seeking the Dharma. "Birth in the Pure Land" is a symbol of becoming part of the Sangha. Amida Buddha created the Pure Land *specifically* for the inferior. For the inferior, the Pure Land is indispensable. The power of the Pure Land means the power of the words of Buddhist predecessors. It is through "listening to their words alone" that one can realize Buddhahood. The only thing necessary for birth in the Pure Land, the land of *Namu Amida Butsu*

(Bowing Amida Buddha), is "bowing." Only a bowing person—a person who knows his own evilness and ignorance—can be born in the Pure Land.

No matter how capable a seed may be, it cannot sprout by itself. If a seed is placed on a rock, it will never sprout. It must have conditions such as heat, moisture, and light. The Pure Land (the Sangha) is the condition that enables us to sprout. It is by receiving power from the Pure Land, from the Sangha, that we can sprout and eventually bear fruit.

Realistically speaking, among the Three Treasures (i.e., the Buddha, the Dharma, and the Sangha), the Sangha is the most important. Becoming a member of the Sangha, of a living tradition, is the most important thing in Buddhism. It is the Sangha that enables us to gain insight into the Buddha and the Dharma. Thus Shin Buddhism says that birth in the Pure Land (the Sangha) is the most important thing. Our birth in the Pure Land, our becoming part of the Sangha, is our liberation.

# 6

# Shinran's View of
# the Two Types of Birth

## Introduction

Birth in the Pure Land (which means spiritual liberation experienced in this life) is one of the most important issues in Shin Buddhism. I want to talk about this issue by discussing Shinran's view of the two types of birth in the Pure Land.

In the Pure Land scriptures the Pure Land is presented as a place that consists of three types of "adornment" (which is defined as "symbolism" by Rev. Ryōjin Soga): (1) the adornment of Amida Buddha, the teacher of the land; (2) the adornment of bodhisattvas, the seekers of Buddhahood; and (3) the adornment of things in the environment, such as land, buildings, and trees. The Pure Land is also presented as a place that is devoid of suffering and full of happiness.

Shinran talks about two types of birth in the Pure Land: "provisional birth" and "true birth." When people suffer, they, on the basis of their dualistic ideas, usually hate suffering and desire to be born in a happy land, either in this life or in the life after death. Shinran calls this type of birth, the type that people usually seek, "provisional birth." He believes that people should move from such birth to another type of birth, "true birth," where they transcend their dualistic ideas and experience oneness—where they can accept the reality of human suffering and see deeper meaning in it.

According to Shinran, since people initially cannot think of any ideal place without using their deluded (or dualistic) ideas, Shakyamuni gave them symbolic descriptions of the Pure Land which conform to their deluded (or dualistic) way of thinking, as an expedient means to guide them to a deeper experience of spiritual liberation. But if people take the symbolically described Pure Land literally as a physical reality and desire to be born there, such a birth is "provisional birth." However, Shakyamuni's real intention was to guide them to "true birth"—to true liberation in which they transcend their deluded ideas and realize true oneness. Now let me explain "provisional birth" and "true birth."

## What Is "Provisional Birth"?

According to Shinran, the best example of "provisional birth" is found in the *Meditation Sutra*,[32] one of the three basic *sutra*s of the Pure Land tradition.

The *Meditation Sutra* contains the story of a tragedy that takes place in the city of Rajagrha. Vaidehi, a queen in the story, experiences tremendous agony; she desires to be liberated from her suffering by seeking birth in the Pure Land.

Vaidehi's suffering starts when Ajatasatru, her son, imprisons the king, his father, with a desire to kill him and usurp his kingdom. Having discovered that Vaidehi, his mother, is carrying food to the king in prison, Ajatasatru gets angry and imprisons her, too. Now, having experienced great despair, she calls upon Shakyamuni for help and says, "I do not want to live in this world filled with all kinds of evil. I want to be born in a place where no suffering exists."[33] Then Shakyamuni teaches her practices, such as visualization and chanting, which are designed to bring about her birth in the Pure Land.

Shinran considers the type of birth that Vaidehi desires "provisional birth." The above words she uttered to Shakyamuni express both her hate of this world of suffering and her longing for a land that does not have suffering. Although her desire for birth is quite sincere, it is still based on her deluded (dualistic) ideas, on her self-centered desires and expectations. Here her attachment to her deluded (dualistic) ideas is not yet challenged or negated.

We are no different from Vaidehi. When we have difficulties in life, we long for a world, either in this life or in the life after death, where no suffering exists. But such a world is always a projection of our egoistic desires. Many Buddhist teachers point out the mistake contained in this orientation. They point out the mistake in our idea that the Pure Land is a place where we can have our individual comfort and pleasure. For example, T'an-luan says, "If people hear that they will constantly experience pleasure in the Pure Land and desire to be born there because of that, they will not be born there." With these words, T'an-luan indicates that the kind of birth in the Pure Land that is conceived on the basis of our deluded (dualistic) human expectations is "provisional birth," not "true birth."

## What Is "True Birth"?

What, then, does Shinran mean by "true birth"? Shinran believes that "true birth" in the Pure Land means "birth in the spiritual realm of the Innermost Aspiration." He believes that the descriptions of the Pure Land found in *sutras* are actually symbolic expressions of the Innermost Aspiration. Since a good understanding of the meaning of the Innermost Aspiration is indispensable for our understanding of Shinran's view of "true birth," let me discuss it.[34]

The Innermost Aspiration means the most ancient desire, or the ultimate desire, which is the basis of human existence. It means the desire to become a Buddha, an Awakened One. The meaning of the Innermost Aspiration, the desire to become a Buddha, is explained in the personal symbol of Dharmakara (or Amida Buddha) in the *Larger Sutra*. Dharmakara shows us the process by which the Innermost Aspiration is first awakened and eventually fulfilled.

Although Dharmakara takes up various practices to realize his Buddhahood, the practice called the visitation (*kuyō*) practice[35] most clearly shows us the Innermost Aspiration that Dharmakara symbolizes. In this visitation practice Dharmakara goes out to revere innumerable Buddhas in the ten directions. The number of Buddhas he worships increases as he intensifies his practice. This way, he eventually comes to view all sentient beings as Buddhas, having transcended his dualistic ideas, such as enlightened and deluded, good and evil, and pure and impure. Through the visitation practice, Dharmakara fulfills his Innermost Aspiration, becomes a Buddha by the name of *Namu Amida Butsu* (Bowing Amida Buddha), and realizes the Pure Land. The Pure Land is the spiritual realm in which the Innermost Aspiration is perfected; the Aspiration pervades every corner of the land.

Now let us see how "true birth" in the Pure Land is described in the "Verses about the Eastern Direction (*Tōbō-ge*)"[36] in the *Larger Sutra*. These verses describe innumerable bodhisattvas who are born in the Pure Land from the eastern direction.

When those bodhisattvas are born in the Pure Land, Amida tells them that they share the same Innermost Aspiration that he has. He tells them that they will unfailingly fulfill their Innermost Aspiration; they will become Buddhas and create their Pure Lands that are no different from his own Pure Land. Then in order to perfect the Innermost Aspiration, those bodhisattvas engage in the visitation practice, the same practice that Dharmakara performed to become a Buddha, and go out of the Pure Land to visit innumerable Buddhas. After having visited and studied under them, they return to Amida's Pure Land. This way, they perfect their Buddhahood by traveling back and forth between Amida's Pure Land and innumerable Buddhas.

Amida, whose essence is an ever-expanding spirit, does not allow bodhisattvas to make their comfortable dwelling place in the Pure Land. He encourages them to forget about their dualistic ideas, to go out of the Pure Land, and to learn from all sentient beings, regarding them as Buddhas. This way, the *Larger Sutra* talks about "true birth" as birth in Amida's Innermost Aspiration—in the spirit that endlessly goes out of the Pure Land to seek oneness with all sentient beings.

In the volume called "Attainment" in the *Kyōgyōshinshō,* the main work of Shinran,[37] Shinran talks about the powerful lifestyle of a person who has experienced "true birth" (whom Shinran calls a *shinjin* person). Shinran says that the *shinjin* person is equal to the highest bodhisattva (that is, like Maitreya), whose main concern is to leave the Pure Land and return to the world of human suffering to realize oneness with all sentient beings in it.[38]

## Mr. A's Entrance into Professor B's Mind

In order to further explain the two types of birth, let me tell a story about Mr. A, a high school student who desires to enter a college. The college that Mr. A desires to enter is famous for Professor B. Mr. A has heard of the professor's reputation, and he desires to study under him. Mr. A believes that the college is a wonderful place where he can perfect his knowledge. Then, Mr. A passes the entrance examination and enters the college.

Now the school begins and Mr. A goes to Professor B's class. Mr. A is thinking that Professor B's instruction in the class will perfect his knowledge. But, as soon as Professor B comes to the class, he tells his students, "The ultimate goal in learning does not exist here in this class, in this college. The most important thing that you students must learn about is the reality that exists outside the college. Here you must learn the importance of your fieldwork. You must go out of this college and appreciate the things and people in the real world. Although you may think that this college and the real world you have left behind are two different worlds, that's not so. If you truly understand my instruction, you will understand that the real world is part of this college—it is an extension of this college. The only important thing about your education here is that you can learn the importance of fieldwork. So you must travel back and forth between this classroom and your fieldwork."

These challenging words of the professor come to Mr. A as a surprise—as a shocking and challenging lesson, because Mr. A has been thinking that the college is the only place where he can perfect his knowledge and the world outside the college is not the place for learning. Now Mr. A must revise his view. According to the professor, the real world that he has left behind is actually the most important place for learning and it is to that world that Mr. A must return.

I have composed this story in order to explain the two types of birth. In this story, "provisional birth" means Mr. A's initial entrance into the college. Mr. A mistakenly thought that his goal was to be found in the college and his knowledge would be perfected there. "True birth" means Mr. A's second entrance, his entrance into the mind of Professor B. It means Mr. A's appreciation of Professor B's view that the most important thing is fieldwork outside the college. Although Mr. A initially thought the goal was to be found in the college, he now realizes that it is to be found in fieldwork.

## Samsara Is Nirvana

Now let me talk about our issue from the perspective of Mahayana Buddhism, whose basic teaching is "samsara is nirvana."[39] The true Pure Land is a place where we learn that "samsara is nirvana"—this reality of suffering is actually an ideal. When we start to study Buddhism, we think nirvana exists outside samsara. Thinking this way, we seek nirvana outside samsara. But Shinran calls such an escapist approach "provisional birth." It is a birth that is based on our dualistic expectations.

But when we meet Amida Buddha, or more specifically, when we meet historical human beings who embody the Innermost Aspiration, they challenge our desire to settle in a comfortable land; they teach us that we should move out of our type of pure land (i.e., "provisional land") and appreciate this world of suffering as part of the true Pure Land. They teach us that samsara is the only place where the Innermost Aspiration can exist and work. The Innermost Aspiration is the spiritual force that is continuously transforming this world of suffering into the Pure Land. It is the spiritual force that is continuously Pure-Land-izing impure lands.

One common Buddhist joke is as follows: A person visits the Pure Land with a desire to meet Buddhas and bodhisattvas. But when he arrives at the Pure Land, he is disappointed because he cannot find any Buddha or bodhisattva there. He is told that all Buddhas and bodhisattvas have gone to impure lands, since they are interested not in staying in the Pure Land, but in visiting impure lands. The minds of impure lands, of deluded people, are interested in going to the Pure Land. But the minds of the Pure Land, of awakened ones, are interested in going to impure lands.

## Conclusion

Initially we are taught that Buddhism is a way of intense self-examination. When we are told that, we think that we must be alone and self-focused, and that we must seek our individual liberation. Thus because of our dualistic ideas, we imagine a wonderful place where we can enjoy individual comfort, pleasure, and happiness. Then in order to attain birth in such a place, we take up various practices, such as meditation and chanting. Shinran calls this kind of birth "provisional birth." Many people stay in this orientation throughout their lives and never recognize the deep self-love that is at the basis of this orientation.[40] We must recognize the mistake in this approach and move to "true birth."

"True birth" means our birth in the Innermost Aspiration—in the spirit that endlessly goes out of the Pure Land. Amida is a symbol of the humble person who endlessly bows his head before all sentient beings, regarding them as Buddhas. His mind is so humble and empty that it can encompass all Buddhas in the ten directions. His mind is filled with his adoration for all Buddhas in the ten directions.

Thus in one verse in his *Hymns of the Pure Land* (*Jōdo Wasan*), Shinran says, "Taking refuge in the Pure Land of Amida means taking refuge in all Buddhas [in the ten directions]."[41] Here Shinran is talking about "true birth." He says that taking refuge (or being born) in Amida's Pure Land means taking refuge (or being born) in Amida's Innermost Aspiration, where Amida is humbly revering all sentient beings as Buddhas. The content of Amida's Buddhahood is nothing but all Buddhas in the ten directions. This also means that those who attain "true birth" in the Pure Land will emulate what Amida did to become a Buddha; they will endlessly go out of the Pure Land and revere all sentient beings as Buddhas.

To Shinran, "true birth" means receiving the power of the Innermost Aspiration (*hongan-riki*) and going back to the reality of human suffering. It means discovering new and deeper meaning in the reality of human suffering. The reality of human suffering becomes, for him, a wonderful place in which he can witness the working of Amida's Innermost Aspiration, and in which he can transcend his dualistic ideas, such as good and evil, and secular and religious, and appreciate oneness with all sentient beings.

# 7

# What Is the Other Shore for the Swallow?

## —*The Happy Prince* by Oscar Wilde—

## Introduction

"The other shore" is a Buddhist symbol: a realm of utmost happiness. In Buddhism we are expected to leave "this shore," the land of suffering, and go to the other shore. People interpret the other shore in many different ways. For example, some interpret it as a place where their desires are satisfied, and others as a place where their desires are eliminated. Some interpret it as a world where they go after they die, and others as a world they attain in this life.

Although people conceive many versions of the other shore, I believe that there are basically two types of other shore: (1) a place where our individual (or self-centered) desires are satisfied; (2) a place where we can transcend our individual (or self-centered) desires. I believe that the latter is the true Buddhist meaning of the other shore.

### The Story of the Happy Prince

To prepare ourselves for a discussion of what I consider the true Buddhist meaning of the other shore, let me present here an outline of *The Happy Prince* by Oscar Wilde. Although this is a fairy tale, I believe that it contains many profound Buddhist messages.

Wilde starts this story this way: "High above the city, on a tall column, stood the statue of the Happy Prince. He was gilded all over with thin leaves of fine gold, for eyes he had two bright sapphires, and a large red ruby glowed on its sword-hilt."

Everybody in the town admired this statue for its beauty and brilliance. One day, a swallow happened to fly into this town. He was in quite a rush. His swallow friends had already gone south to Egypt six weeks before. This swallow had been fooling around with his girlfriend and had forgotten all about the passing time. Suddenly, he realized that winter was about to come. He realized that he must leave for the south, too; otherwise he would die in the cold weather.

Thus the swallow flew all day long, and at night he arrived in the town. Then he looked for a place to pass the night. He found the statue of the Happy Prince and perched on its foot. When he was about to fall asleep, a large drop of water fell on him. He thought it was rain. But the water that fell on the swallow was actually a teardrop from the eyes of the Happy Prince.

The swallow asked, "Who are you?" The Happy Prince answered, "I'm the Happy Prince." The swallow asked, "If you are the Happy Prince, then why are you crying?" The Happy Prince answered:

> When I was alive, I did not know what tears were. I was living in a palace. Everything around me was so beautiful. There were all kinds of pleasure and happiness around me. People called me the Happy Prince. There was a lofty wall around the palace and I never cared to ask what lay beyond it. So I lived, and so I died. And now that I am dead, they have set me up here so high that I can see all the ugliness and all the misery of my city. I cannot help but weep.

Then the prince continued, "There is a poor house over there. A thin and tired woman is in the house. In the bed her little boy is ill. The boy is crying because of his sickness and hunger. Swallow, swallow, little swallow, will you not bring her the ruby out of my sword?"

The swallow answered, "My friends are waiting for me in Egypt. They are having a nice time in the warm weather there. I must go there, too." The prince said, "Swallow, swallow, little swallow, will you not stay with me for one night, and be my messenger? The boy is so thirsty, and the mother is sad."

Since the prince looked so sad, the little swallow was sorry. He thought, "What's the difference? Only one night! All right. I'll do it." So he decided to stay with the prince for one night to be his messenger. The swallow picked the ruby out of the prince's sword and took it to the poor house.

The next day, the swallow thought he should not waste any more time and should leave the town immediately. When he went to the prince to say good-bye, the prince said, "Swallow, swallow, little swallow, will you not stay with me one more night?" The swallow said, "Another night! O, prince, how dare you ask something like that? My friends are having a nice time in the warm weather in Egypt and are waiting for me."

The prince said, "I see a poor young man. He is trying to finish a play for the theater. But he is too cold to write any more. There is no fire in the house and hunger has made him faint. So please stay with me one more night and be my messenger." Since the prince looked so sad, the swallow decided to stay one more night. Since there was no longer a ruby on his sword, the prince asked the swallow to pluck out one of his sapphire eyes and take it to the poor young man.

On the third day, the swallow went to the prince and said, "I have come to say good-bye. I must leave now." The prince said, "Swallow, swallow, little swallow, will you not stay with me one more night?" The swallow said, "O, again! Dear prince, how dare you ask something like that? It is already winter, and the chill snow will soon be here. In Egypt, the sun is warm. My friends are building their nests and are bringing up their baby swallows. O, dear prince, let me go." The prince said, "In the square below there is a little match girl. She has just dropped her matches into the gutter. If she does not bring any money home, her father will beat her. She is crying. She is trembling from the cold and she is hungry."

Finally the swallow said, "All right. I'll stay with you one more night." Then, he plucked another sapphire eye from the prince and took it to the poor girl. When the swallow came back, he said to the prince, "You are blind now, so I will stay with you forever." Surprisingly, the swallow said, "I'll stay with you forever."

From the next day on, when the swallow saw poor starving people, he reported what he saw to the prince. And the prince asked him to take off the fine gold leaves that covered his body and take them to the poor people. As the swallow picked off one gold leaf after another, the statue of the Happy Prince began to look quite dull and gray.

Then the snow came. The little swallow grew colder and colder. And at last he knew that he was going to die. He had just enough strength to fly to the prince's shoulder one more time. He said, "Good-bye, dear prince." Then the swallow kissed the prince and fell down dead at his feet.

The next morning, the mayor of the town saw the statue and said, "How shabby the Happy Prince looks! The ruby has fallen out of his sword, his eyes are gone, and he is no longer golden. In fact, he is little better than a beggar. And there is even a dead bird at his feet." So the people pulled down the statue of the Happy Prince and threw it away with the dead swallow.

### What Is the Other Shore for the Swallow?

Now let me return to our topic of the other shore. Let me ask my readers, "What is the other shore for the swallow?" Probably some of my readers will answer, "The other shore for the swallow is Egypt. Egypt is the land of happiness that he really wants to go to."

Yes, it looks like that. It looks like Egypt is the other shore for him. The swallow is so eager to go to Egypt. He thinks his happiness is to be found in Egypt. But is Egypt really the true other shore, the land of true happiness, for him? I do not think so. In the story, the swallow thinks, "If I were in Egypt, I would have warm weather. If I were in Egypt, I would have such a nice time." He is dreaming of all kinds of wonderful things in Egypt. By using subjunctive expressions, he is dreaming all kinds of dreams. But his dreaming is endless. In the north the swallow dreams about his happiness in the south. In the south he dreams about his happiness in the north. There is no end to his dreaming.

Similarly, we frequently say things like "If I could get into a nice college, if I could get employed by a nice company, if I could get married to a nice person, if I had a nice family, if I had a nice retirement, if I could be born in a nice world after death..." How many ifs have we had in our past? How many ifs do we have now? How many ifs are we going to have in our future? We have an endless continuation of ifs. I do not think our true happiness can be found in relying upon this endless continuation of ifs, of dreaming. In the case of a swallow, moving from one place to another is called migration. In the case of human life, moving from one dream to another is called transmigration (samsara).

"The other shore" is a symbol of utmost happiness in Buddhism. "Going to the other shore" means *putting an end to the endless cycle of transmigration.* It means *putting an end to our continuous dreaming.* It means terminating our attachment to our future-centered (or goal-oriented) way of thinking and living. Our future-centered way of thinking and living is called "this shore." Going to the other shore means becoming firmly settled in full appreciation of what we have here and now.

I do not think that Egypt is the true other shore for the swallow. Egypt is still a component of his migration, of his transmigration. Then what is the true other shore for the swallow? I believe that it is the Happy Prince. Initially the swallow thinks he has to go to Egypt to realize his happiness; but in meeting the Happy Prince, he experiences a deep joy and happiness that he has never experienced before. He finds a greater way of finding fulfillment than going to Egypt. I believe that his entering into the compassionate spirit of the Happy Prince is his going to the other shore.

### Shinran's Meeting with His Teacher Hōnen

This story by Wilde reminds me of Shinran's meeting with his teacher Hōnen. Shinran was like the swallow in the story. Shinran went to Mt. Hiei when he was eight. After that, for about twenty years, Shinran studied and practiced Buddhism there. On Mt. Hiei Shinran attempted to attain the other shore (or Buddhahood). But in spite of the desperate efforts Shinran was making, he was unable to attain his goal.

But when Shinran was twenty-eight, he met Hōnen, who embodied the Innermost Aspiration—the spirit of Amida Buddha. The Innermost Aspiration means the desire to become one with all sentient beings, to go into the midst of suffering people and share their suffering. Hōnen was not concerned with such matters as his own individual comfort, pleasure, and happiness. He lived among ordinary people, such as samurais, merchants, and farmers, and identified himself with them.

Having seen the Innermost Aspiration in Hōnen, Shinran was deeply moved by it. Having recognized the mistake he was making in his Buddhist approach, Shinran became ashamed of himself. He now realized how self-centered he had been in his search for Buddhahood. Shinran realized that he had been dwelling in a tiny religious cocoon of his own making. In the cocoon, he was dreaming all kinds of Buddhist dreams. He was dreaming of his type of other shore.

Just like the swallow who realized that his true other shore existed not in Egypt but in the prince, Shinran realized that his true other shore existed not in what he had imagined to be the other shore but in the Innermost Aspiration that Hōnen embodied.

For both the swallow and Shinran, there were two types of other shore. Their provisional other shore was the world that they imagined. Their true other shore was the Innermost Aspiration that they witnessed in the human beings they met.

## Conclusion

I want to finish this essay by discussing how going to the other shore, or entering into the Innermost Aspiration, can be realized in our lives. Although we may think that we have the Innermost Aspiration in our beings and can awaken it by ourselves, the Innermost Aspiration is so deeply hidden in us that we cannot. It is only when we meet a person who embodies the Aspiration and we experience spiritual resonance with that person that we can have our Innermost Aspiration awakened within us.

Initially the swallow was not aware he had the Aspiration. When he met the prince, it was awakened in him. Then the swallow realized that the Aspiration was not only an external reality but also an internal reality. When the prince said, "Swallow, swallow, little swallow," his voice was coming not only from outside but also from within the swallow. Thus the voice had enormous power. The swallow could not resist the voice because it was a command that was coming from within the deepest part of his being.

We can say the same thing about Shinran. When he met his teacher Hōnen and experienced spiritual resonance with him, his Aspiration was awakened in him. When Shinran met Hōnen, he heard the voice of the Innermost Aspiration. The voice was coming not only from Hōnen, a teacher outside himself, but also from within, from the deepest part of his being. Thus the voice had tremendous power. Shinran calls it "an absolute command from the Innermost Aspiration."[42]

It is crucially important that we meet a human being who embodies the Innermost Aspiration. Once we have deep spiritual communion with that person, we will never forget it. We will unfailingly embark on a life that is rich, creative, and fulfilling. We will live the powerful lives of constant seekers who are not afraid of our own evil passions, or the reality of suffering. We will find creative meaning in everything we experience in our lives. Shinran talks about this in the following verse:

> Having met with the power of the Innermost Aspiration,
> None of us passes his life in vain.
> Our life becomes the treasure ocean that is filled with
>     wonderful qualities.
> The defiled waters, our evil passions, are now an inseparable
>     part of the treasure ocean.
>
> —*Hymns of Great Monks*[43]

# 8

# The "Priceless Jewel" within Us

## Introduction

In this essay I want to talk about the importance of going inward and discovering a "priceless jewel,"[44] something perfect, that exists within us. Dr. Kitarō Nishida (1870–1945, a famous Japanese philosopher) says that there are two types of religion in this world. He calls them "religions of external transcendence" and "religions of internal transcendence." Christianity is a religion of external transcendence and Buddhism is a religion of internal transcendence. In Christianity, people go out of human existence and seek God, something perfect, outside it. In Buddhism, we go into human existence and discover something perfect in ourselves.

Buddhism does not allow us to seek an external (divine) savior. It teaches us to thoroughly examine ourselves through the words of our teachers and recognize our deludedness. It is in the process of self-examination that we can transcend our deludedness and discover the "priceless jewel" that exists within ourselves.

I will first discuss the nature of our deludedness. Then, I will talk about our teachers, Shakyamuni, Shinran, and Mrs. Hisako Nakamura, who discovered the "priceless jewel."

## Human Deludedness

People usually think that something is missing or lacking in themselves. They think they must go outside themselves to seek it. Seen from the perspective of Buddhism, this way of thinking is called human deludedness or upside-downness.

The following two illustrations show us the deludedness of seeking something outside ourselves. In the *Surangama Sutra* we read the following story.[45]

Once there was a handsome young man by the name of Yajnadatta. He loved his own handsome face; every morning he looked at it in a mirror and admired it. But when he looked into the mirror one morning, he could not find his face. He was so upset; he thought he had lost his face. So he went out to look for it. He frantically asked people, "Did you see my face somewhere? Did you see my face dropped in the street?" Then, people started to laugh at him and said, "Yajnadatta, what are you saying? You have your face right there. You haven't lost it at all." Then, Yajnadatta went home and checked the mirror. He discovered that he was looking at the wrong side of the mirror, so he could not find his face there and thought that he had lost it.

There is another story about a Chinese poet. One day the poet looked at a calendar and learned that it was the first day of spring. Believing that there must be some sign of spring somewhere, he went out to find it. All day long he walked through hills and valleys to find a sign of spring. But he could not find any. Tired, he went home. He thought, "Spring has not come yet; the calendar must be wrong." Then he sat at the entrance of his house and looked down. There he found a tiny flower starting to blossom. He said, "Oh, here is a sign of spring. I didn't have to go out to a faraway place to discover it. It's here right in front of my house."

These two stories tell us that although the two men, Yajnadatta and the poet, already had what they needed in the places closest to them, they thought they did not have it and went out to search for it. Buddhism teaches us that we are precisely like them. In spite of the fact that we already have something perfect in the places closest to us, we think we do not have it and go out to search for it in the external world. Simply because it is so close to us, we cannot discover it. Buddhism is not a teaching about creating a new reality or world. It is a teaching about discovery, immediate discovery of the "priceless jewel" that we already have within us here and now.

## Life

What, then, is the "priceless jewel" that we already have within us here and now? Buddhism teaches us that it is life. Life is simply so close to us that we have not fully discovered and appreciated it. "Life" is such a common word, an ordinary word that we use all the time. It may not sound like a profound religious or Buddhist concept. But there is no greater or deeper religious concept.

When Shakyamuni attained Buddhahood, he simply discovered life. He simply discovered that he was life—that he had always been life. Shakyamuni's becoming a Buddha means that he became awakened to what he already was. He did not create a new reality. He just discovered the reality that was already there.

We usually say that he discovered the truth of impermanence. But the truth of impermanence is synonymous with life. The truth is that all things in this world, not only animate things but also inanimate things, are alive. They are manifesting the constant newness and freshness of life.

Shakyamuni discovered the truth of life, or impermanence. This truth is also called *tathata* ([original] suchness), because it was already there whether Shakyamuni was aware of it or not. The realization of his Buddhahood just means that he became aware of the truth. Thus, he compared himself to a traveler who discovered an ancient city that already existed.

## Something Perfect in Shin Buddhism

Now let me discuss the same issue specifically within the context of Shin Buddhism. How does Shin Buddhism talk about this "priceless jewel" of life?

The *Larger Sutra* has the story of Bodhisattva Dharmakara's becoming a Buddha, a mythological story. Dharmakara initially made vows to become a Buddha and create a Buddha land. After a long period of practice, he became a Buddha by the name of Amida Buddha and created a Buddha land called the Pure Land ten *kalpa*s—a long, long time—ago.

Dharmakara desired not only the realization of his Buddhahood and creation of his land but also all sentient beings' birth in his land. He wished that if he realized his Buddhahood and his land, all Buddhas in the ten directions would praise him by calling his Name; the words of their praise would resound throughout the universe. And all sentient beings that listened to the words of praise and desired to be born in his land would be born there immediately.

Thus the *Larger Sutra* says that ever since Amida created the Pure Land, he has been calling all sentient beings to be born there. This calling voice of Amida reaches all sentient beings, assuming the form of words of praise from all Buddhas in the ten directions, our historical teachers.

This story of Amida's creation of the Pure Land teaches us that something perfect, a perfect world, was already created a long time ago. It teaches us that the most important thing for human beings was *already perfected* a long time ago. Thus it shows us that the only important thing for us to do is not to create a perfect world, but to listen to the calling voice (i.e., the words of our historical teachers) coming from the perfect world. It is to discover the perfect world and return to it, to be born in it.

Then, what is the perfect world that concepts such as Amida Buddha and the Pure Land symbolize? Amida Buddha and the Pure Land symbolize life, the truth of impermanence, or the truth of original suchness. Amida is a symbol of limitless life; and the Pure Land is a symbol of the world of limitless life. And we are inherently life, and part of limitless life. Amida, limitless life, is calling us to awaken to it through the words of our historical teachers. It is waiting to be heard and discovered.

## Shinran's Experience

Mahayana Buddhism teaches us that all human beings could and should become Buddhas. When we are told to realize Buddhahood, many of us think that we must create Buddhahood, or a new world, for ourselves. But that, I believe, is a misunderstanding of Buddhism. Becoming a Buddha means becoming awakened to life, or to the truth of impermanence, which already exists. The story of Amida's creation of the land of limitless life ten *kalpa*s ago means that we do not have to create a new reality or world. The perfect world already exists and we have only to be born into it.

Let me talk about Shinran here. When Shinran was eight years old, he went to Mt. Hiei. Then he attempted to become a Buddha. Through various practices he attempted to perfect himself and create his own new world. But he had a hard time attaining his goal. Then he, being frustrated and depressed, started to doubt the validity of the practices that he was performing. However, when Shinran was twenty-eight, he met Hōnen, who made him recognize the mistake in his approach. As I would put it, Hōnen said to Shinran, "Shinran, you do not have to perfect yourself. You do not have to create your own Buddhahood or your own new world. Amida (limitless life) already exists. Something perfect already exists. You are already being embraced by it. You are already part of it. The entirety of your being, including all your flaws and imperfections, is part of something perfect. Just listen to the voice that is coming from Amida. He is telling you, 'Come immediately as you are!' Just wish to be born in his land!"

Before Shinran met Hōnen, he thought that he had to perfect himself and create something perfect. But now he recognized his mistake. He did not have to create anything perfect. Something perfect was already there. It had been there all the time. Amida, limitless life, had been there all the time. Shinran realized that the only important thing for him to do was to listen to the calling voice that was coming from the perfect world, to awaken to it, and to be immediately born into it.

He realized that his belief that he could perfect himself and attain Buddhahood through his own efforts was actually his greatest hindrance, because it prevented him from listening to the calling voice. When he recognized the futility of reliance upon his own efforts, he was able to clearly listen to the calling voice.

He also realized that the perfect world was given equally to all people, the good and the evil, the wise and the foolish, and the young and the old. All people could be immediately born into this world without any moral requirements or intellectual qualifications. Thus Shinran experienced immediate liberation (birth in the Pure Land) by listening to the calling voice that was coming from the perfect world; he discovered that he was embraced by this wonderful world.

## Mrs. Hisako Nakamura

There was a famous Shin follower in Japan by the name of Mrs. Hisako Nakamura (1897–1968).[46] When Mrs. Nakamura was three, she lost all four of her limbs because of frostbite. In those days in Japan, a disabled child was a shame for the family. Thus during her childhood, she was raised in the family closet and kept away from the public. When she grew up, she earned her living in a circus by showing how she could write and sew with her mouth. This lasted twenty-two years. Her life was not easy.

In her later years, however, she became a Shin Buddhist and appreciated Shinran's teachings. There is one memorable poem she wrote. In Japanese, the title of the poem consists of three identical words, *"aru aru aru."* In English it means, "I have it, I have it, I have it."

Although we might think that there were many things missing and lacking in her life, she says that she discovered something wonderful and perfect in herself. She discovered a world in which she could be perfectly happy and content. She expressed her joy at discovering this wonderful world with this poem that says, "I have it, I have it, I have it." We usually feel something missing and lacking in ourselves and go out to search for it. We usually think, "I don't have it, I don't have it, I don't have it." But she said, "I have it, I have it, I have it."

## Conclusion

A few days before Shakyamuni passed away, he was traveling toward Kushinagara where he would die. When he looked at the evening sky, he said to Ananda, "Ananda, this world is so beautiful, so wonderful."

When Shakyamuni said those words, he certainly knew that this world had not only all kinds of joy and happiness but also all kinds of suffering and tragedy. But, he said, "This world is wonderful" in spite of all the suffering and tragedy. No, to use the expression "*in spite of* all the suffering and tragedy" here is not appropriate. It would be more correct to say that he said, "This world is wonderful" precisely *because of* all the suffering and tragedy.

There are two types of human happiness: situational happiness and existential happiness. Situational happiness means the happiness that one experiences when a favorable situation or condition satisfies a specific need or desire. Existential happiness means the happiness that one experiences when he appreciates the truth that is inherent in his existence—the ever-abiding truth of life or impermanence, regardless of the nature of his situation or condition. When Shakyamuni said, "This world is beautiful," he was talking about existential happiness.

When we reflect upon our lives, we realize that we have been searching for situational happiness—for things outside ourselves. Since childhood, we have been searching for external objects and goals such as a good education, a good job, a good marriage, and a good family. Some of us have been searching for external saviors such as gods and Buddhas. We have been doing so because we felt something was missing and imperfect in ourselves and have not been able to find perfect contentment within.

But we must ask ourselves, "Do we not have something perfect within ourselves? Do we not have something with which we can be perfectly happy and content here and now?" The answer, I believe, should be, "Yes, I have it, I have it, I have it."

Our teachers such as Shakyamuni and Shinran teach us that we already have something perfect in ourselves. They teach us that we have enough reason to be happy at any time and in any place, and that we have bottomless depths within us. It is not God that is inconceivable and unfathomable. It is human existence. Buddhism is nothing but a teaching about awakening to the bottomless depths in human existence.

Things that we have acquired from outside will wear off. Things that we have put on from outside will peel off. We cannot take our fame and fortune to our graves. All the information, knowledge, skills, and scholarship we have acquired will be gradually lost as we get older, as our memories get weaker. But there is one thing that does not age and disappear. It is the ever-abiding truth of impermanence—limitless life. This truth is always new and fresh. Symbolically, it is called Amida. Amida, limitless life, is calling us to awaken to it at the depths of our being. It is so wonderful to discover that we are part of this dynamic and creative reality. This discovery makes us so happy, so grateful.

The *Larger Sutra* says that Amida created the Pure Land ten *kalpas* ago and has been calling us to be born there ever since. This story teaches us that the most important thing for us was *already perfected* a long time ago. It is already given to us here and now. Something quite profound, quite wonderful, is already given to us. We are already part of it. We do not have to create a new world, a perfect world. We do not have to augment or decorate our existence from outside. We have only to discover this perfect world, to return to it, and to be born into it.

# True Practice

# 9

# Not Practice, But Understanding

People usually say that it is easy to understand but it is difficult to practice. These are words of secular sentiment. They are words of untruth. The words of truth are quite the opposite: "It is difficult to understand, but it is easy to practice." If we can truly understand, then action will naturally follow. Action that is not based on understanding is simply deluded action. And how can we easygoingly say that the understanding in "understanding the truth" is an easy matter? Understanding is indeed difficult. Buddhism as a teaching of the truth, or as an intellectual religion, maintains the position, "Understanding is difficult, but practice is easy."... Shinran says that among the difficult the most difficult is "genuine understanding (*shin*)." He talks about "*Shin* that is the most difficult (*gokunan-shin*)."

— Shūichi Maida[47]

In order to understand this unique feature of Buddhism, that it primarily emphasizes understanding (or wisdom), not practice (or discipline),[48] let us first examine the process by which Shakyamuni attained enlightenment.

After six years of ascetic practice—an attempt to eliminate passions through self-discipline—Shakyamuni renounced it. Having left this practice, he started to meditate under a tree. Simply meditating under a tree was not considered a full-fledged practice in his time. Thus the co-practitioners whom he had left behind mocked him, saying, "Siddhartha has become a backslider and taken to an easier lifestyle." But it was this meditation, which seemed an idle action to the religious practitioners of his time, that led Shakyamuni to enlightenment.

What, then, was the meditation that Shakyamuni took up under a tree and that led him to enlightenment? It was "understanding"—understanding of the self. He was desperately asking one question, "What am I?" He wanted to understand the basic nature of the self, because he thought that his ignorance—his lack of understanding—of the self was the basic cause of suffering and that by clearly understanding the self, he could eliminate suffering.

In examining the basic nature of the self, Shakyamuni investigated whether there was something permanent in the self. After intense introspection he came to the conclusion that all things that made up the self were impermanent. That is, he recognized that not only physical elements such as muscle and blood but also mental elements such as volition and consciousness were constantly moving and changing. He recognized that impermanence was the only Dharma, the only absolute reality (or truth) underlying his existence.

In this way he clearly discovered the cause of suffering and the way to eliminate it. He identified ignorance of the self (or misunderstanding of the self as something permanent and substantial) as the cause of suffering. Although the basic nature of the self was impermanence, he was attached to the self; he considered it permanent and desired to maintain it against the truth. Thus friction between his self-attachment and the truth was inevitable. This friction was the suffering he was experiencing.

But when Shakyamuni understood the absoluteness of impermanence, he recognized the mistake in his self-understanding. Now he totally identified with the truth of impermanence and loosened his grip on the self. Then the friction between the self and the truth disappeared. He experienced liberation from suffering. This insight into the truth of impermanence was the content of Shakyamuni's enlightenment. It was by this insight alone that he became a Buddha.

As soon as Shakyamuni recognized that his entire being was impermanence itself, he identified himself with it. He became the truth and started to live his life as the truth. His "understanding the truth (or awakening)" was simultaneously his "becoming the truth."

Now a few words on the meaning of "becoming the truth." Although "becoming the truth" may sound like Shakyamuni had just become the truth, that is not the case. Its true meaning is this: Shakyamuni, who had always been the truth of impermanence but had not been cognizant of it, became awakened to the fact that he had always been the truth of impermanence. In that sense, he recovered (or discovered) what he really was rather than newly becoming what he had not been before. Thus "becoming the truth" was contained in "understanding the truth."

In this way his "understanding the truth" contained in itself a total (both mental and physical) transformation of his life. Although "understanding" is usually construed only as mental transformation, his understanding was so thorough that it brought about total transformation of his life. Thus his mental transformation was simultaneously physical transformation.

Hence in Buddhism, "understanding" and "practice" cannot be discussed as two separate issues. Practice, which is usually identified with the physical (or lifestyle) aspects of human life, cannot be discussed in isolation from understanding the truth. Practice is fully contained in understanding the truth.

When we attain right understanding, right practice—a lifestyle that is based on the truth of impermanence—is simultaneously attained. Thus all our efforts in Buddhism should be focused on gaining right understanding, not on disciplinary practices. No matter how many disciplinary practices we may take up, they do not guarantee our attainment of right understanding. But attainment of right understanding immediately guarantees the attainment of right practice.

# 10

# Tradition and Creativity

*I rejoice in what I have heard.*
*I praise what I have received.*
—Shinran, the *Kyōgyōshinshō*[49]

## Introduction

Tradition and creativity appear to be opposites. Honoring tradition means honoring the old values of the past, whereas creativity means the destruction of the old values of the past and the production of new values. When we are honoring a tradition, we are passive, focusing our attention on the past. But when we honor creativity, we are active, focusing our attention on the future. Then how can we synthesize these two seemingly conflicting things? What should the ideal relationship between them be?

Before I discuss this issue, let me talk about one difference that I have witnessed between the Japanese and Americans. As a person who has lived in Japan and in the United States for about equal lengths of time, I have learned that there is a considerable difference between the Japanese and Americans concerning their attitudes toward their own cultures. The difference is this: The Japanese have a good sense of what it means to have a long cultural tradition, whereas Americans do not.

In their respective attitudes toward their cultures we can see both a good point and a bad point. As far as the Japanese are concerned, their good point is that they have considerable respect for their long history and cultural tradition. But this good point is also their bad point. Because they have a long cultural tradition, they are often bound by rigid conventions. They are expected to conform to a cultural pattern. They do not have much freedom. If they desire to be creative and different, they are immediately criticized. A Japanese proverb says, "A nail that stands out will be hit down."

As far as Americans are concerned, their good point is that because they do not have a long cultural tradition, they are not restrained by conventions. They can freely come up with new creations. But this good point is also their bad point. Because they do not have a long cultural tradition, they do not know what it means to have deep respect for tradition.

Thus generally speaking, the Japanese are mainly bent on honoring their traditions and Americans on honoring creativity. But we must say that tradition that is automatically maintained and is not capable of producing new values (which we often see among the Japanese) is a "dead" tradition; and that creativity that is not based on deep respect for a tradition (which we often see among Americans) is not "true" creativity. It is shallow and does not have lasting value.

I believe that the Japanese way and the American way represent two extremes and they must be synthesized. I believe that we must have both deep respect for tradition and deep respect for creativity. Then, what should the ideal relationship between tradition and creativity be? My answer to this question is: First, we must have deep respect for a tradition. Deep respect for a tradition is the indispensable basis of true creativity. It is *only after* we deeply respect a tradition and thoroughly learn from it that we can have true creativity. To speak in extremes, deeply respecting a tradition *is* true creativity.

In this essay let me first talk about the importance of learning from a tradition as the basis of creativity. Then I will discuss the meaning of creativity in Buddhism. Finally I want to discuss the essence of Shinran's doctrine, which, I believe, is nothing but deep respect for tradition.

## Tradition as the Basis of Creativity

Rev. Rijin Yasuda said, "New things are old; and old things are new." By this statement, he meant that the new and fashionable things of our time, such as best sellers, will immediately become old, but old things, such as the classics, are always new. He said that it is a mistake to chase after fashionable things. If we simply chase after new things without learning from the past, the new things will immediately become old. He said that the classics are the source of our creativity and we must learn from them. New creation can only come out of learning the classics.[50]

Shūichi Maida said:

> Lenin said, "Take one step forward and two steps back!"... it is absolutely necessary for us to take two steps back in order to take one step forward. Taking two steps back means good learning. Good learning can make us take a creative step forward. Without good learning, without taking two steps back, we cannot take a creative step forward. If we only think about advancing, we will stumble and fall down. We cannot possibly take a firm, creative, steady step forward... More emphasis should be placed on learning than on thinking of new ideas. Creativity comes quite naturally out of learning.[51]

The Japanese word for "learn" is *manabu*. This word *manabu* derives from another Japanese word, *manebu*, which means "imitate." According to Webster's English Dictionary, the English word "learn" derives from *last* (an old English word meaning "footprint"), or from *lira* (a Latin word meaning "track"). Thus both the Japanese word "*manabu*" and the English word "learn" have similar meanings—"following (or imitating) the footprints of predecessors."

When we think about the education we have received at school and at home, we can understand that learning means imitating and following the footprints of our predecessors, our teachers and parents. Further, when we look at how art students study, we can easily understand that learning means imitating. They spend much time copying the works of great artists. Bashō (1644–94, a Japanese *haiku* poet) said, "First, enter the standard rules and then exit from them."[52] By this he means that it is only after we thoroughly learn from a tradition and imitate and follow it that we can create something new. If we think that we can come up with a new creation without learning from the past, we are totally wrong. Following the footprints of our predecessors is the only basis of creativity. True creativity cannot exist without respect for a tradition, without thoroughly learning from it.

## The Tradition of Honoring Tradition

Now I have discussed how deep respect for a tradition is the basis of creativity. This is one of the main teachings of the *Larger Sutra*.

The *Larger Sutra* talks about a story in which Dharmakara becomes Amida Buddha. When Dharmakara meets a Buddha, his teacher, he awakens his desire to become a Buddha. Dharmakara then expresses his desire to create a wonderful land that has never existed before. Then he asks his teacher to give him instruction concerning how to create the land. The teacher initially refuses to give instruction. He says, "In such a matter as the creation of your land, I cannot help you. You yourself must find the way to do it." But, being moved by the repeated requests of Dharmakara, the teacher gives instruction. The teacher says:

> If one keeps on emptying a great ocean with a pint measure, one will be able to reach the bottom after many *kalpa*s and then obtain a wonderful treasure. Likewise, if one sincerely and diligently keeps on seeking the Way, one will be able to attain one's goal. What Aspiration is there that cannot be realized?[53]

Here the teacher talks about two things: "emptying the ocean" and "obtaining a wonderful treasure." By "emptying the ocean" the teacher means a tedious process of learning—learning from tradition, from predecessors. By "obtaining a wonderful treasure" he means creation of a new land (or the realization of Buddhahood). Here the teacher is instructing Dharmakara that he must first engage in a tedious process of learning from tradition before he can create a new land and become a Buddha.

Then, after receiving this instruction, Dharmakara engages in a practice called eternal practice. In this practice, he visits Buddhas as many as the sand grains of the River Ganges. He worships and serves them. He studies under them. This practice is what his teacher meant by "emptying the ocean." Here Dharmakara keeps on listening to the teachings of innumerable Buddhas—he keeps on following their footprints. Here he is simply honoring tradition.

It was only after "emptying the ocean" (i.e., learning from tradition) that Dharmakara was able to "obtain a wonderful treasure" (i.e., create his own Buddha land and realize his own Buddhahood). This story of Dharmakara teaches us that it is only after we have thoroughly learned from a tradition that we can become truly creative people.

Only the continuously learning spirit, only the spirit that deeply honors tradition, can transform itself into a creative spirit. This creative spirit that is backed by deep respect for a tradition is at the basis of the Buddhist literary tradition. Look at how Buddhist authors wrote their writings. The writings of Indian Buddhist teachers are called *abhidharma*s (commentaries) or *sastra*s (commentaries). They are commentaries or exegeses on *sutra*s. The fact that the writings of those teachers were commentaries means that they had tremendous respect for their tradition, for their predecessors. Those teachers were simply interested in learning from their tradition. They wrote down what they had learned from their tradition.

When Indian Buddhist texts came to China, Chinese Buddhists composed their own writings. The writings of Chinese Buddhists are called *ron-shaku*s (commentaries on commentaries). Chinese masters' writings are commentaries on Indian commentaries. Chinese Buddhist teachers were simply interested in learning from their Indian predecessors.

Buddhist teachers throughout history were not interested in asserting their own ideas, or in showing off their own interpretations. They were just interested in learning from their teachers. That's why their writings took the form of commentaries.

But this does not mean that they were not creative, or that they did not come up with new ideas and interpretations. On the contrary, all those Indian and Chinese Buddhist teachers were very creative people. In the process of thoroughly learning from their predecessors, they were able to come up with new ideas and interpretations. Their new ideas were natural by-products of their deep respect for their predecessors.

Probably one of the best examples of this humble spirit of Buddhism can be seen in Shinran. The *Kyōgyōshinshō*, his main work, is a very unusual book. A recently published English translation of this text consists of about 300 pages. About 80% (240 pages) of the text consists of quotations from *sutra*s and his predecessors' writings; and 20% (60 pages) consists of Shinran's own words.[54] Usually authors write about their own ideas in 80% of the book and have quotations in 20% of the book. Thus Shinran's book is the total opposite of regular books. Shinran's book takes this form because he had tremendous respect for tradition, for his predecessors. His main interest was in learning from tradition. His *Kyōgyōshinshō* was a study notebook. The main purpose of writing it was to collect wonderful passages that he found in the Buddhist literature that had been handed down to him. This is reflected in the full title of the *Kyōgyōshinshō:*

### *A Collection of Passages that Reveal the True Teaching, Practice, and Attainment of the Pure Land [Tradition]*

Collected by Foolish-Baldheaded Shinran,
a Disciple of Shakyamuni

Here Shinran indicates that the text is a collection of passages from *sutra*s and his predecessors' writings. He also says "Collected by Shinran," not "Written by Shinran." He identifies himself as a recipient of the teachings, not as the creator of a teaching. We can see this humble attitude of his in his expression in the preface of the text: "I rejoice in what I have heard. I praise what I have received."

If Shinran was totally devoted to learning from his predecessors, does that mean that he did not develop any new insights, any new ideas in his writings? No, not at all. On the contrary, we can see many new insights, ideas, and interpretations in his writings. All these new insights arose quite naturally as a result of his deep respect for tradition.

**From Tradition to Creativity**

To further discuss how creativity is realized through deep respect for tradition, let me quote the words of Mr. Kōzō Masuda, a famous Japanese chess champion. In a lecture he said, "The spirit of a real pro is the spirit to become greater than his teacher."

Mr. Masuda came up with this statement because he had spent many years in imitating his teacher, had thoroughly digested whatever his teacher offered him, and had attained a level that surpassed his teacher. His words emphasize the importance of transcending one's teacher. They also mean that he has created something totally his own. They are synonymous with Zen expressions such as "When you meet a Buddha, kill him. When you meet a teacher, kill him"[55] and "Take one more step beyond the hundred-foot pole."[56]

Here we can talk about the proverb, "You can take a horse to a river, but you cannot make it drink." We cannot reach a river without the guidance of our teachers. It is absolutely necessary that we trust our teachers, listen to their words, and follow their footprints. Our teachers, however, cannot make us drink the water. When we have thoroughly received their guidance and gotten to the river, we must say "Thank you" to them and depart from them. This departure is called "becoming greater than a teacher" or "killing the teacher."

What, then, does "drinking the water" mean in Buddhism? It means the realization of Buddhahood. What is the realization of Buddhahood? It means realization of the true self. Then what is the true self? It is the Dharma self—the self that is one with the truth of impermanence. The truth of impermanence is the truth of the constant newness of life. It is creativity itself. Thus the true self, the Dharma self, is the self that is creativity itself.

Amida Buddha is a symbol of the true self, the self that is creativity itself. It is a symbol of the self that is one with the constant newness of life—that is continuously seeking and learning. The ultimate goal in Buddhism is to realize the Amida Buddhahood in us—to become a person who can appreciate the newness of life in all existing things, who can appreciate the bottomless depth and richness of his or her own life.

The goal of Buddhism is liberation from all forms of reliance and attachment; it is transcending our attachment to dualism. However, we must know that this goal is attained only when we go through the dualistic process of relying upon our teachers. Initially we must respect our teachers, listen to them, and study under them. All of these actions are dualistic actions, because the teacher-student relationship is itself dualism. But this dualistic process is the only thing that enables us to transcend our attachment to dualism.

Initially there seems to be something graspable in our Buddhist teachers, but we must eventually realize that there is nothing graspable in them. Our teachers teach us to be liberated from all forms of reliance including reliance on themselves. They teach us to discover the true self, the Dharma self, and become ourselves. They are happy if we leave them and become independent.

### Shinran's Emphasis on the Seventeenth Vow

Here I want to briefly explain the basic features of Shinran's doctrine. I have so far discussed the relationship between tradition and creativity. I have said that creativity is realized through deep respect for a tradition. I believe that what I have discussed so far is the essence of Shinran's Buddhism.

Probably the most outstanding doctrinal feature of Shinran's thought, the one that distinguishes him from other Pure Land masters (including his teacher Hōnen), is that he equally emphasized the importance of two vows—the Seventeenth and Eighteenth Vows—described in the *Larger Sutra*.

Hōnen was famous for emphasizing the exclusive importance of the Eighteenth Vow. Following his teacher Shan-tao's interpretation,

Hōnen interpreted the Eighteenth Vow as follows: "If, when I (i.e., Dharmakara) attain Buddhahood, the sentient beings of the ten directions call my Name as few as ten times and yet are not born in the Pure Land, may I not attain the supreme enlightenment."[57] Based on this interpretation, Hōnen considered that because of "calling Amida's Name" he was able to attain birth in the Pure Land.

But Shinran considered that because of "listening to the Name," not because of "calling the Name," he was able to attain birth in the Pure Land. Although Hōnen interpreted the sentient beings' action described in the Eighteenth Vow as "calling [of the Name]," Shinran interpreted it as "listening [to the Name]." Shinran thought that "calling (or praising) of the Name" was found in the Seventeenth Vow, not in the Eighteenth Vow. He also thought that "calling (or praising) of the Name" was done by innumerable Buddhas in the ten directions, not by deluded sentient beings like himself. Shinran believed that deluded sentient beings like himself were immediately born in the Pure Land only through listening to the Name that is being called (or praised) by innumerable Buddhas in the ten directions.[58] (This, however, does not mean that Shinran could not participate in "calling [or praising] of the Name." He thought that if he could truly listen to the Buddhas' calling voice, the calling voice would vibrate his being and spontaneously come out of his own mouth. He believed that since it was a practice given to him from the sphere of Buddhahood, he could not call it his own practice.)

Shinran thought that the Seventeenth Vow talked about the concrete manner in which Amida's Aspiration (i.e., a symbol of the ultimate truth that is beyond words) had become words and teachings—a *logos* tradition in its historical context. The Seventeenth Vow says, "If, when I (i.e., Dharmakara) attain Buddhahood, innumerable Buddhas in the lands of the ten directions should not call (or praise) my Name, may I not attain perfect enlightenment." Shinran interpreted the "innumerable Buddhas" mentioned in this vow as referring to historical teachers such as Shakyamuni and the seven patriarchs. Thus Shinran thought that "innumerable Buddhas' calling (or praising) of Amida's Name" meant the words and teachings of historical teachers such as Shakyamuni and the seven patriarchs—the *logos* tradition that had been transmitted to him. It was only through listening to this *logos* tradition that Shinran could attain birth in the Pure Land (here and now) and eventually attain Amida Buddhahood or *parinirvana* (at the end of his life).

## Conclusion

The uniqueness of Shin Buddhism is that it talks about two Buddhas: Shakyamuni Buddha and Amida Buddha. Shakyamuni Buddha is a historical Buddha; he represents historical Buddhas—historical teachers. Amida Buddha is a symbolic Buddha; he symbolizes the ultimate truth, universal Buddhahood, or our true subjectivity.

To use the two key concepts that I have been discussing in this essay, Shakyamuni Buddha and "tradition" are synonymous; and Amida Buddha and "creativity" are synonymous. The goal of Buddhism is to realize the Amida Buddhahood (true subjectivity) in ourselves. It is only by honoring the tradition, only by listening to the words of the historical teachers represented by Shakyamuni, that we can realize the Amida Buddhahood in ourselves.

By emphasizing the importance of the Seventeenth Vow, Shinran eliminated ambiguous and somewhat mystic elements that existed in previous Pure Land teachings and made it clear that the only important thing in Buddhism was to listen to the words of predecessors. "Listening" was everything for Shinran. It was not a means of liberation. It was itself liberation. Thus we can see in Shinran the development of a doctrine in which honoring tradition is everything; it leads to the realization of the true self that is creativity itself.

# 11

# Absolute Passivity

## Introduction

I want to talk about the importance of absolute passivity in Buddhism. We usually emphasize the importance of being active in Buddhism—of actively engaging in various actions and practices. Certainly actions and practices are important in Buddhism. But it is quite crucial to know that the awakening (or enlightenment) that is the core experience in Buddhism is an extremely passive experience.

Individuals such as Shakyamuni and Shinran lived their lives in the most dynamic and creative way. When we read their biographies, we tend to think that they always lived like that. But that was not the case. There were moments of absolute passivity in their lives. And it was the moments of absolute passivity that were the basis of their dynamic and creative lives. Unless we gain insight into the absolute passivity that they experienced and we, too, experience the same type of passivity, we cannot be said to be truly studying Buddhism; we cannot experience the same awakening.

## The Passivity in Shakyamuni's Life

Let me first discuss the absolute passivity that Shakyamuni experienced. Tradition tells us that after Shakyamuni left his palace and became a seeker, he spent six years studying various doctrines and performing various practices such as yoga and meditation. He even took up ascetic practices. But he had serious doubts about those practices. He thought that there was still religious self-love at their root. Thinking that it was impossible to attain liberation through practices that were based on religious self-love, he abandoned them.

When Shakyamuni renounced those practices and received a pot of milk from a maiden to recover his strength, his co-practitioners thought that he had failed and ridiculed him, saying, "You have become a backslider and taken to an easier lifestyle."

Then Shakyamuni sat under a tree to meditate. Then what does it mean that he sat under a tree? It means that he became passive, having removed himself from all active attempts to seek liberation. His sitting under a tree was a symbol of passivity. Now, he became an empty receptacle that could be immediately filled with the Dharma.

Now Shakyamuni realized that the most important thing in the path to enlightenment was not his religious practices, not his attempts to change himself into a new being, but an immediate recognition of the Dharma, the truth of impermanence. The Dharma was life itself. It was the dynamic truth, the constant newness and freshness of life. It was there all the time, but he had not been aware that it was. Now he was ready to hear the voiceless voice of the Dharma that had been calling him. It was constantly telling him, "Awaken to what you really are! Awaken to the fact that your entire being is nothing but the truth of impermanence! You are nothing but life! Discover the wonderful reality, the dynamic reality, that exists at the basis of your being!" Having listened to this voice, Shakyamuni was liberated; he became a Buddha—an embodier of the Dharma.

In this moment of absolute passivity Shakyamuni experienced both the death of his old self and the birth of his new self. When he recognized the absoluteness of the Dharma of impermanence, he saw the emptiness of the self that he had cherished. This was his experience of the death of the old self. Then, he simultaneously saw another new self being born in him—the self that was permeated with the Dharma. Now he recognized that the Dharma was the only reality in his being. Thus, from the time Shakyamuni attained enlightenment until he died at the age of eighty, he lived his life in a powerful and creative way, being one with the Dharma.

I believe that the content of Shakyamuni's enlightenment was his Dharma-listening at that moment of absolute passivity. Dharma-listening alone liberated him. The term Buddha means an "Awakened" One. The grammatical form of this word Buddha ("Awakened") is the past passive participle. It means that Shakyamuni was *awakened* (or *liberated*) by the Dharma. Shakyamuni never said that he could take credit for his enlightenment; it was the Dharma that awakened and liberated him. He was a passive recipient of the Dharma.

## The Passivity in Shinran's Life

Now let me talk about Shinran. When Shinran was eight years old he went to Mt. Hiei and started to study Buddhism there. During the next twenty years Shinran engaged in traditional Buddhist practices such as self-discipline and meditation. He attempted to attain Buddhahood through those practices. But, as was the case with Shakyamuni, Shinran gradually developed serious doubts about those traditional practices. Shinran also detected the religious self-love that was at their root. Thus he came to the conclusion that self-love based practices could not possibly achieve the selflessness that he was seeking.

When Shinran was twenty-eight years old, he could no longer continue his practices and stopped them. He realized that he was a total failure as a religious practitioner. His words in the *Tannishō,* "Since I am incapable of performing any religious practice, hell is my only home," succinctly show us the despair that he was feeling at that time.

Having discontinued his practices, Shinran became passive. It was, however, in moments of passivity that he met Hōnen. Shinran saw that the essence of Hōnen was the Innermost Aspiration. For Shinran, the "Innermost Aspiration" and "Amida Buddha (i.e., a personal symbol of the Innermost Aspiration)" were synonymous with the Dharma, the ultimate reality or truth. According to the teaching of the *Larger Sutra*, the Innermost Aspiration meant "the aspiration to transcend the dualistic way of thinking (i.e., the thinking that compares good and evil, pure and impure, happiness and unhappiness)." It also meant "appreciating all things that one encounters in this life as indispensable conditions for the fulfillment of one's life." When Shinran met Hōnen, he encountered the Innermost Aspiration. Thus Shinran describes his meeting with Hōnen with the words: "I have abandoned miscellaneous practices (i.e., practices based on the dualistic way of thinking) and taken refuge in the Innermost Aspiration."[59] Having met Hōnen, a person who embodied the Innermost Aspiration, Shinran was deeply moved.

When Shinran met Hōnen, he heard the voice of the Innermost Aspiration speaking from him. It said, "Shinran, you don't have to perfect yourself. You don't have to make yourself good and pure by eliminating evil and impurity from your being. Know the pettiness of your criteria for good and evil, purity and impurity! Forget about them! Forget about your calculating mind, your dualistic mind! It is all right to be what you are. A perfect world already exists. Something perfect, the Dharma, already exists. You are already being embraced by it. The entirety of your being, including all your flaws and imperfections, is part of the Dharma reality, the wonderful reality. Nothing in your life is meaningless or wasteful. Even what you consider evil and impure has meaning. It is an indispensable component of your life. Just awaken to the fact that you are already being embraced by the Dharma reality!"

Before Shinran met Hōnen, he thought that he had to perfect himself. But now he recognized his mistake. He did not have to perfect himself. Something perfect was already there. It had been there all the time. The Dharma had been there all the time. The voice of the Dharma, the Innermost Aspiration, was telling him to transcend the pettiness of the dualistic way of thinking. It was telling him that everything in his life, even his evil and foolishness, had meaning. Now he accepted the entirety of his being. He realized that he did not have to change or improve his being; the only important thing for him was to listen to the voice that was coming from the perfect world and immediately discover the fact that he had already been embraced by it.

This way, Shinran experienced both the death of his old self that relied on the dualistic way of thinking and the birth of a new self that was permeated by the power of the Innermost Aspiration.

Now having been filled with the power of the Innermost Aspiration, Shinran started to live his life in a dynamic way.

We have seen that both Shakyamuni and Shinran, having lost faith in the self-based way, became total failures as religious practitioners, stopped their practices, and became passive. When they became passive, they became perfect listeners; they were able to listen to the voiceless voice of the Dharma. The crucial moments in the lives of Shakyamuni and Shinran were absolutely passive moments. It was in those moments that they were penetrated by a new power and were transformed into new Dharma-permeated beings.

**Active Grabbing and Passive Receiving**

In both Shakyamuni and Shinran we can see that when their hands were actively grabbing at enlightenment, they failed to attain it. But when they saw the futility of their attempts to grab it, they stopped their attempts and their hands became passive. Then, enlightenment came to them.

Here let me discuss the importance of passivity by giving a couple of illustrations. First, I want to talk about how to catch dragonflies. When I was a small boy in Japan, catching insects was one of my hobbies. If I actively reached for dragonflies, they immediately flew away. It was not easy to catch them that way. But there was an easy way to catch them. It was to stop reaching for a dragonfly and just to stick out one of my fingers and keep it still. If I did so, a dragonfly would come to perch on my finger. Then I just held its legs and caught it. I believe enlightenment is just like a dragonfly. If we try to reach for it, it will go away. But if we become passive, it will come to us. If we become perfect listeners, it will be heard by us.

I can say the same thing about artists. Many first-class artists say that their art is not so much creation of new things as discovery of what already exists. It is true that seen from outside, artists look as though they are making efforts to create new things. But, as far as their internal awareness is concerned, many of them feel that they are actually witnessing and appreciating something that already exists.

Great painters would say that they are witnessing the beauty that already exists in nature. They would say that nature is offering the beauty to them; they are just receiving it and recapturing it in their canvases. Great musicians would say that they are listening to the sounds that already exist in this world. They would say that this world is offering the beautiful sounds to them; they are just listening to them and reproducing them. We may think that activity (or being active) is at the core of creativity, but it is passivity that is at the deepest core of creativity.

This reminds me of a story about Michaelangelo, the famous Renaissance artist. One day Michaelangelo and his disciples were walking. They came across a huge marble rock. Then Michaelangelo said to his disciples, "A beautiful Venus is sleeping in this marble rock. She is asking me to rescue her from it." None of his disciples could see the image of Venus in the rock. But Michaelangelo could see it. He asked his men to transport the rock to his workshop. Then he carved a beautiful image of Venus out of the rock. For Michaelangelo beauty already existed in the rock. He was like a midwife whose work was assisting the birth of an unborn life.

## Two Types of Practice: Self-initiated Practice and
## Dharma-initiated Practice

Here I want to discuss the two types of practice that we can see in the lives of Shakyamuni and Shinran. The first practice is the practice that they actively performed before they experienced absolute passivity, and the second practice is the practice that they performed after they experienced absolute passivity. In other words, the first practice is self-initiated practice, and the second practice is Dharma-initiated practice. The first practice is practice we perform relying upon our own abilities; and the second practice is practice in which the Dharma (or the Innermost Aspiration) is working in us. We can call the first practice "our" practice, and can take credit for it; but we cannot call the second practice "our" practice and we cannot take credit for it.

In the initial stage of our study of Buddhism, we all engage in the first practice, self-initiated practice. We engage in religious activities such as self-discipline and meditation. This is an important and necessary stage, but it is a preliminary stage beyond which we must go. If we seriously pursue this initial stage, there will be moments in which we start to see some basic mistakes contained in the practice and we will stop it. Then there will be a moment of absolute passivity. Just as Shakyamuni and Shinran stopped their self-initiated practices, we must stop our self-initiated practices. Just as Shakyamuni and Shinran became passive listeners, we must become passive listeners.

Then, we realize that there is a wonderful reality that already exists. We further realize that the wonderful reality is telling us to forget about our petty dualistic way of thinking—that nothing in our lives is meaningless. It is telling us that it is all right for us to be what we are. When we hear the voice and experience awakening, we become new beings. Our self-initiated living becomes Dharma-initiated living.

## Conclusion

Let me conclude this essay by discussing the Zen master Dōgen's view of enlightenment. In his work entitled the *"Kōan* of Present Becoming (*Genjō-kōan),"* Dōgen says that people initially make all kinds of efforts to attain enlightenment, but their self-conscious efforts to attain it become a hindrance. So long as we are thinking that *we can attain* enlightenment, we cannot do so because the idea that *we can attain* it becomes a hindrance. There is deep religious self-love there. When we come to see the total futility of the self-initiated way, we stop it. We lose faith in our self-initiated way and become humbled and passive. This is a mature moment. It is also a moment of tremendous opportunity. Now the Dharma can penetrate us. Dōgen says that true enlightenment is not the experience of *our attaining* the Dharma; it is rather *the Dharma's attaining us* or *our being attained by the Dharma.*[60]

In the lives of our predecessors such as Shakyamuni and Shinran, we see moments of absolute passivity. It was in moments of absolute passivity that they listened to the voiceless voice that was coming from the Dharma, the ultimate reality. Having listened to the voice that said that it was all right for them to be what they were, they accepted what they were and became themselves. That was their enlightenment and liberation.

Unless we, too, experience total disillusionment about our self-based way and experience absolute passivity, we cannot listen to the voice that is coming from ultimate reality. Initially we think we can take credit for all our actions. But that is an immature and shallow way of thinking. Our activity must turn into passivity. Buddhism teaches us to experience a passivity in which we move from the self-initiated way to the Dharma-initiated way.

# 12

# Two Types of Practice in Shin Buddhism

## Introduction

"Practice" is one of the most intriguing issues in Shin Buddhism. I have met many Shin Buddhists who were totally confused about what "practice" means in Shin Buddhism. They told me, "When I attend traditional Shin Buddhist services like the Hō-onkō (Shinran's memorial service), speakers often tell us that there is no practice in Shin Buddhism and that the *nembutsu* ("saying the Name of Amida Buddha") is not a practice. But when I attend other services like the Ohigan ("[Going to] the other shore [through the six practices]"), speakers tell us that the six *paramita* practices[61] are important, because they enable us to go to the other shore, the sphere of enlightenment, and we should perform them. Since speakers give us two totally different teachings concerning practice, I am really confused. Does Shin Buddhism have a practice? Or does it not have any?"

If I give an answer to this question, it is as follows: Shin Buddhism talks about two types of practice—"wrongly determined" practice and "rightly determined" practice. When we say that there is no practice in Shin Buddhism, that means that there is no "wrongly determined" practice in Shin Buddhism. And when we say that there is a practice in Shin Buddhism, that means that there is a "rightly determined" practice in Shin Buddhism. To further explain these two types of practice, let me tell a story.

## The Story of a Lost Boy

One day a father and his son go hiking in a forest. Initially they are walking together. Since the boy was born and raised in a city and has never been out in a forest, he is very much excited to see birds, flowers, and insects in the open air. He enjoys picking up flowers. He chases after butterflies. Then the boy gradually walks away from his father. He goes deeper and deeper into the forest. And he finally gets lost. His father realizes that his boy is lost, so he starts shouting, "My boy, where are you? Are you lost? Come back here! Listen to my voice and come back!" But the father cannot hear any response.

The boy is so excited about everything he sees in the forest that he is not aware he is lost. Then, it gets darker and darker and he gradually realizes that he is lost. When he knows this, he becomes desperate; he starts to look for the way. But he cannot find it. The more he runs around to look for the way, the deeper into the forest he goes. After running around, the boy gets exhausted. Being unable to find any more power in himself and not knowing what to do, he just sits there on the ground, crying. He is in deep despair. He believes that he will die there.

So far the boy has been listening to his own voice, which has told him, "Go this way! Go that way!" Now that voice has stopped coming. His mind has become empty. It has become totally passive. Now for the first time his listening is turned toward the outside. Then something happens; he hears a voice coming from outside himself. He realizes that his father is calling him. Having recognized his father's voice, he feels a new power gushing out of his being. He stands up and rushes toward the voice. And he gets rescued.

## The Three Stages in Lostness

Here I want to talk about the three stages in the boy's lostness. The first is the stage in which the boy, having recognized his lostness, desperately seeks a way to get out of his miserable condition. The second is the stage in which he, having become totally exhausted, gives up his efforts to look for the way; he sits hopelessly on the ground. The third is the stage in which he hears his father's calling voice and, being urged by his innermost desire, rushes toward it and gets rescued.

We can find these three stages in Shinran's life. Shinran calls the first stage "wrongly determined (or falsely settled)," the second stage "indeterminate (or unsettled)," and the third stage "rightly determined (or truly settled)."[62]

The first stage, which Shinran calls "wrongly determined," refers to the twenty years that Shinran spent on Mt. Hiei. There he desperately attempted to get out of the world of delusion, or lostness, by performing all kinds of religious practices. By relying upon his dualistic way of thinking (*ji-riki*), he attempted to eliminate his evil passions and become a Buddha. Although he tried hard to attain Buddhahood, he was unable to do so. On the contrary, Buddhahood seemed far away; he became more and more confused and depressed. He developed deep doubts about those practices.

The second stage, which Shinran calls "indeterminate," refers to the time in which he hit a dead end in his practices and became totally passive. He came to the conclusion that although he had spent twenty years on Mt. Hiei, the practices there could not lead him to liberation. He experienced total exhaustion, despair, and frustration. This was the time when he realized, "Since I am incapable of performing any religious practice, hell is my only home." Although this was an experience of total disillusionment with himself, it was an important stage for him. It made Shinran become totally passive. Without experiencing this total passivity, he would not have been able to enter the third stage.

The third stage, which Shinran calls "rightly determined," begins at the time when he met his teacher Hōnen. When he met Hōnen, he heard the calling voice of the Innermost Aspiration that told him to recognize the pettiness of his dualistic way of thinking. Hōnen was a channel through which the voice was coming. When Shinran listened to it, he was immediately liberated and experienced tremendous joy. He was permeated by the power of the Innermost Aspiration. Thus, he started to live a dynamic and creative life.

## Two Practices: Wrongly Determined Practice and Rightly Determined Practice

Just as the lost boy experienced the two types of going (i.e., the desperate going in the first stage and the joyous going in the third stage), Shinran experienced two types of going or practice—"wrongly determined" practice and "rightly determined" practice.

According to Shinran, the difference between these two types of practice is as follows. The first practice is practice that is done on the basis of the self—with one's own dualistic (or calculative) way of thinking. The second practice is practice that is done by listening to the Innermost Aspiration—by listening to the voice telling one to transcend the dualistic way of thinking. We can call the first practice "self-initiated" and the second practice "Dharma-initiated" (or "Aspiration-initiated").

Thus, what differentiates these two practices is whether one truly listens or not. Meeting a teacher and listening to him is extremely important in Buddhism. Shinran says that listening alone is necessary; he does not talk about a need for any other practices. In Shin Buddhism the most important awakening experience is called *shinjin* ("awakening [realized through listening]"). Selflessly listening to the teachings of his predecessors and receiving the power of the Innermost Aspiration from them were the most important spiritual experience as far as Shinran was concerned. Actually the greatest dignity in human existence is that we *can listen to* the teachings of our teachers. All human beings, be they good or evil, wise or foolish, young or old, healthy or sick, rich or poor, can listen. They can listen to the Dharma any time, at any place.

## Two Ways of Traveling the Bodhisattva Path

When Shinran was performing the first practice, the basis of his practice was his religious self-love, or his attachment to the dualistic way of thinking. The basic nature of the first practice was such that he had to force himself to perform it. Here, his practice meant a whole bunch of "shoulds" and "shouldn'ts." It meant that he "should take" wholesome actions (such as giving, self-discipline) and that he "shouldn't take" unwholesome actions (such as killing, stealing, and drinking).

But when Shinran met his teacher and listened to the voice of the Innermost Aspiration, he started to engage in the second practice. It was practice initiated by the Innermost Aspiration. The nature of his practice went through a total transformation. He no longer had to force himself to perform various practices. The difficulties that existed in the first practice completely disappeared. Now the joy of listening and gratitude for the teachings of his teachers became the basis of his practice. "I should do it" turned into "I cannot help doing it." "I shouldn't do it" turned into "I cannot waste my time in doing it."

In the first practice, Shinran had a hard time in traveling the bodhisattva path, in performing the six *paramita* practices (i.e., the perfections of [1] giving, [2] discipline, [3] patience, [4] effort, [5] concentration, and [6] wisdom). But in the second practice, thanks to the power of the Innermost Aspiration, they were now effortlessly realized in him.

The meanings of the six *paramita* practices went through a total transformation in Shinran's life. Initially Shinran had to force himself to practice giving, but now giving was effortlessly realized in him. He felt that since he was receiving so much from the world, he could not help sharing it with others. Initially he imposed disciplines upon himself, but now he felt that he did not have to impose it. It was effortlessly realized in him. He now enjoyed Dharma-listening so much that he could not waste his time in doing things that are called "breaking precepts." He felt that he had to make the best use of his time and energy for Dharma-listening. Initially he forced himself to be patient, but now he felt that the joy of Dharma-listening made him endure things that he could not endure before. Initially he forced himself to make an effort to study the Dharma, but now he enjoyed Dharma-listening so much that he did not have to make an effort to do it. Initially, he forced himself to concentrate his mind, but now concentration was realized naturally, because he had a focus in his life—Dharma-listening and appreciation of the power of the Innermost Aspiration. Initially, he strove to perfect his wisdom, but now he received wisdom (i.e., *shinjin*) from his teachers in the process of Dharma-listening. He did not have to strive to attain wisdom.

## Shinran's View That a *Shinjin* Person Is the Same as the Highest Bodhisattva

I have explained the difference between the two types of practice which Shinran teaches. Now I want to discuss one of his most remarkable teachings. It is his teaching that when "a foolish ordinary person (*bompu*)" whose body is filled with evil passions attains *shinjin*, he can be, just as he is, elevated to the stage of the highest bodhisattva. Shinran says that the power of the Innermost Aspiration is so powerful that it immediately makes such a person transcend samsara. This is Shinran's unique teaching, which we cannot see in other Pure Land masters, including his teacher Hōnen.

Shinran identifies the attainment of *shinjin* with the attainment of "birth in the Pure Land," "the rightly determined stage," "the stage of non-retrogression," and "the stage of *samyak-sambuddha* (which immediately precedes the stage of perfect Buddhahood)."

Shinran says that a *shinjin* person will never go back to his samsaric way of living, will live his life in the most powerful way, being filled with joy and gratitude, and will attain *"parinirvana"* or "the stage of perfect Buddhahood," the final goal of Buddhism, at the last moment of his life.[63] Shinran believed that the physical death of a *shinjin* person is the completion point, a full stop; it will be the attainment of *parinirvana* (which literally means "complete extinction or combustion [of one's life]") or the attainment of perfect Buddhahood, which means "the completion of human life."

Shinran says that although a *shinjin* person, being full of evil passions, does not deserve to be called a bodhisattva, he, due to the great power of the Innermost Aspiration that he has received, immediately transcends samsara and is elevated and enthroned to the rank of bodhisattvahood. Let me cite here three texts in which Shinran identifies a foolish ordinary person with a bodhisattva.

In his work called the *Gutoku's Notes,* Shinran comments on the "traveler" in the parable of "The Two Rivers and White Path."[64] Shinran says that the traveler who has experienced *shinjin,* having listened to the words of Shakyamuni Buddha and Amida Buddha, although his "desires are countless, and anger, wrath, jealousy, and envy are arising within him without pause to the very last moment of his life"[65] is "a bodhisattva who is definitely assured of attaining perfect Buddhahood."[66]

In his work called *Hymns of the Two Gates of Entering and Exiting,* Shinran says that the person who has attained the "mind of diamond *(shinjin)*" no longer belongs to the group of foolish ordinary persons:

> The foolish ordinary person who fully possesses evil passions
> Is encompassed by the power of the Buddha's Aspiration
>     (or Vow).
> Such a person no longer belongs to the group of foolish
>     ordinary persons.
> Such a person is a white lotus among people.[67]

In his work called *Hymns of the Three Dharma Ages,* Shinran identifies the *shinjin* person with Bodhisattva Maitreya, a figure who symbolizes the stage of *samyak-sambuddha* (which immediately precedes the stage of perfect Buddhahood):

> Bodhisattva Maitreya must pass 5,670,000,000 years
> Before attaining Buddhahood,
> But the person who receives true *shinjin*
> Will attain Buddhahood at the end of his life.
>
> The person who reaches *samyak-sambuddha*
> By the power of the Vow designed for [sentient beings']
>     birth through the *nembutsu,*
> Being the same as Maitreya,
> Will attain *parinirvana.*[68]

Although Shinran identities the *shinjin* person with Bodhisattva Maitreya, he is actually saying that the *shinjin* person is superior to Maitreya. Shinran says that although Maitreya is a person of "gradual transcendence," the *shinjin* person is a person of "immediate transcendence." Although Maitreya must wait a long 5,670,000,000 years before he attains perfect Buddhahood, the *shinjin* person, having attained the stage of Maitreya through the power of the Innermost Aspiration (or Vow), will realize perfect Buddhahood at the end of his life. To this extent, Shinran emphasized the importance of one's meeting with the power of the Innermost Aspiration. Shinran believed that everything important in Buddhism is immediately resolved by meeting with this power, and tremendous joy and happiness are experienced through that meeting.

## Conclusion

I have talked about the two types of practice discussed by Shinran—the first practice (wrongly determined practice) that is based on the dualistic way of thinking and the second practice (rightly determined practice) that is based on the power of the Innermost Aspiration. Shinran's meeting with the power of the Innermost Aspiration was the crucial point that made Shinran move from the first practice to the second practice.

In contrast to most Pure Land masters of Shinran's time, who sought birth in the Pure Land after death and regarded their present life as the place where they prepared themselves for birth in the Pure Land after death, Shinran's main concern was fully traveling the bodhisattva path in this life and realizing *parinirvana* or perfect Buddhahood, i.e., the goal of the bodhisattva path, at the end of his life. When Shinran met his teacher and encountered the power of the Innermost Aspiration, he found the way. He started to live his life powerfully and creatively, being permeated by this power. He says that it was so tremendous that the fact that he had evil passions was no hindrance to his living the dynamic and creative life of a bodhisattva.

Shinran describes himself as evil, foolish, and incompetent.

When people read these negative self-descriptions, they may think that Shinran, having found no power within himself, just depended upon the external saving power of Amida Buddha. But such an interpretation is wrong. His negative self-descriptions and the joy that he was experiencing in his meeting with the power of the Innermost Aspiration were two sides of the same coin. It was the wonderful and positive qualities of the power that permeated him that made him see the negative qualities in his being. It was the joy and happiness in appreciation of this power that made him recognize the negative qualities in his being. When we read Shinran's negative self-descriptions, we must hear his shout of joy at the same time — the joy of being able to live a powerful and creative life. Further, in talking about various wonderful spiritual qualities of the *shinjin* person, Shinran says that "he has all kinds of excellent virtues"; "he is full of joy and gratitude"; and "he is constantly performing the great (Buddha's) compassion."[69]

# General Topics

# 13

# What Is a "Buddhist"?

*All views are perverted views. No view is the right view.*

*—Prajna-paramita Sutra*

Ever since I came to this country from Japan, I have noticed one major difference between American Buddhists and Japanese Buddhists. The difference is that American Buddhists like to identify themselves as Buddhists, saying, "I'm a Buddhist," whereas, in Japan people seldom identify themselves as Buddhists. As a matter of fact, when I lived in Japan I never said to my friends, "I am a Buddhist."

Every time I hear Americans identify themselves as Buddhists, I have a mixed—comfortable and uncomfortable—feeling about it. I have this mixed feeling because I sense in their words both admirable and erroneous elements. Let me talk about these two elements.

First, the admirable element is this: Americans identify themselves as Buddhists because they take Buddhism seriously, whereas, many Japanese do not do so because they do not take Buddhism seriously. They regard Buddhism only as part of their traditional culture; they do not regard it as a personal religion. But, for some Americans, Buddhism is a personal religion, an exciting new religion in which they wish to be personally involved. This is an admirable element I see in American Buddhists.

Now let me discuss what I consider an erroneous element. I feel uncomfortable when I hear people identify themselves as Buddhists because I sense some kind of religious pride or arrogance. The majority of people in this country are Christians. Thus people who take up non-Christian religions have a sense of rivalry with

Christianity. Some of them believe that Buddhism is superior to Christianity. In order to assert their superiority they say that they are Buddhists, not Christians. But if people use the word "Buddhist" to feel superior to others, they are doing something unjustified in Buddhism—something totally against Buddhism. Buddhism does not allow us to be attached to any form of label or identity, or to indulge in any form of self-love or self-enhancement.

I am not saying that we should not identify ourselves as "Buddhists." It is all right to do so. But we must have a clear idea as to what we mean by the word. What, then, is a "Buddhist"? When we say we are Buddhists, how are we viewing other religions such as Christianity? What kind of attitude are we taking toward them?

Since I cannot adequately discuss these questions without referring to my personal background, let me talk about it. In my life, three individuals have exerted considerable spiritual influence on me. I consider them my teachers. Let me start with the first teacher.

When I was a junior high school student, I met a teacher, Mr. Keisuke Itō. Mr. Itō had difficult experiences when he was young. During World War II he was a Japanese soldier and was put into a Russian concentration camp in Siberia. He was forced to engage in hard labor there. I heard that many of his friends starved to death. Because of this difficult experience in Siberia, he became a Christian. After he came back to Japan, he became a schoolteacher. Mr. Itō was so different from other teachers. When he taught the class, I could tell that he was searching for meaning in his own life. He often challenged us to reflect upon our lives. He usually looked depressed and gloomy. So, many classmates of mine, young teenagers who loved cheerful teachers, did not like him at all. He was too serious for them. But somehow I was attracted to this teacher. Since I was very young at that time, I do not think I fully understood him. But I was deeply impressed by the serious manner in which he was teaching us. Because he was a Christian, I became interested in Christianity.

Now let me talk about my second teacher, whom I met when I was a high school student. Since Mr. Itō, a Christian, impressed me, I started to attend a Christian church when I was in high school. One day, I attended a class for young adults in this church. There were several high school boys and girls. As I was attending a boys' high school, and the boys were quite rough, I needed to see some girls at least once a week; this was absolutely necessary for my mental health.

During the class, one cute girl asked me, "Mr. Haneda, what kind of novelist do you like best?" This was a tough question, because in those days I was interested only in baseball and fishing. I was not academically inclined at all; I had not read any significant books. But a really cute girl was asking me the question. I had to impress her. I could not say, "I don't read any books." If I had said so, it would have sounded so dumb. So, I seriously thought "What have I read, what have I read?" Then, I remembered that I had read one short story by Lev Tolstoy. So, I told her, "Yeah, I, of course, like Lev Tolstoy. He wrote *War and Peace* and *Anna Karenina*." (Although I had never read these novels, I knew he wrote them.) She was very much impressed. So it was okay at that time. But it was not okay after that, because she thought I was a specialist on Tolstoy and started asking me various questions about him. So, I had to read Tolstoy. I rushed to a bookstore and bought *War and Peace* and *Anna Karenina*, huge books. (I really thought that I should have told her that I loved O. Henry or Jack London. They would have been much easier to read.) But, I said "Tolstoy," so I had no choice. Initially I forced myself to read Tolstoy. Then, gradually I started to love Tolstoy. So when one year had passed, I was more in love with Tolstoy than with that girl. Although Lev Tolstoy is commonly known as a novelist, he was actually a very religious person. When he was around fifty, after he wrote *Anna Karenina*, he experienced a so-called religious conversion. Most of his later writings were religious writings. I consider Tolstoy my second teacher. So, when I chose my major in college, I chose Russian. I wanted to be a translator of Tolstoy.

Now let me talk about my third teacher. I was in college in the late sixties. In 1969 I was a senior. One day I went to a bookstore and bought a commentary on Goethe's *Faust,* a famous German story. The author's name was Shūichi Maida. I had never heard of him. When I read the commentary on *Faust*, I was really impressed, not by the story of *Faust* but by what the commentator Maida said about *Faust*. Although I had not known it, the commentator was a Buddhist and was interpreting *Faust* from a Buddhist standpoint. In the book Maida used many Buddhist terms, such as Amida Buddha, Shakyamuni, and Shinran. Up to that time, I had no interest in Buddhism at all. To me Buddhism had been part of our obsolete culture. But the Buddhism that I found in Maida was so fresh, new, and relevant to my life. Then, I went back to the same bookstore and bought other books written by him. I started to study Buddhism at that time. That was the turning point in my life. From that time on, for the last thirty years, I have been studying Buddhism.

Now I have talked about the three teachers, Mr. Itō, Tolstoy, and Maida. If I describe them with traditional labels, they are quite different. Mr. Itō was a Christian. Tolstoy was a Russian novelist. Maida was a Buddhist. But in my mind, I cannot differentiate these three people. They form what I am today.

A friend of mine once asked me, "Mr. Haneda, how did you make the switch? How did you switch from Christianity to Buddhism and from Russian literature to Buddhism?" When I was asked this question, I did not know how to answer it because I did not feel that I had ever made a switch from Christianity to Buddhism or from Russian literature to Buddhism.

By getting to know Buddhism, I came to have a deeper appreciation of Christianity and Russian literature. I do not see any conflict between studying Christianity and Buddhism, or between studying Russian literature and Buddhism. Actually, studying Christianity and Russian literature is part of my study of Buddhism. For me, studying Buddhism does not mean reading the so-called "Buddhist writings" per se. It means studying all kinds of things, such as Christianity and Russian literature.

To me, Buddhism means realizing an all-embracing *attitude*, nothing else. It means realizing a broad and empty mind that can encompass all. It means realizing a position in which I can learn and appreciate all kinds of things—a position in which I do not assume any relative or antagonistic relationships with them.

I can talk about this with a simple illustration. Suppose there is a basket that contains all kinds of fruits such as an apple, an orange, a peach, a pear, etc. To me, religions that have fixed dogmas or creeds are like the fruits in the basket. We can compare these religions just as we can compare the fruits in the basket. But Buddhism is not a fruit in the basket; it is itself the basket that holds all kinds of fruits. Buddhism has no fixed dogma, creed, or doctrine. If Buddhism had that, then it could be compared with another dogma. But Buddhism does not have any dogma or creed that can be compared with any other. We can compare an apple with an orange, or an orange with a peach. But we cannot compare an apple with a basket.

Here some people may disagree with me and say that there are doctrines, ideas, and concepts in Buddhism. Yes, there are certainly ideas and concepts that are taught in Buddhism. But they are not "fixed" doctrines to be attached or carried around by us. They are cures for sickness. They are something like Drano that is used to eliminate a clog in a pipe. When water regains its smooth and natural flow, Drano is no longer necessary. Buddhist ideas and concepts are antidotes against the poison of human attachment. Since we are attached to various objects, Buddhist teachers challenge us with ideas such as "impermanence" and "emptiness" and destroy our attachments. These ideas are totally different from the dogmas that many other religions have.

Let me discuss the basic meaning of "Buddhism" or "Buddhist" by referring to the famous parable about five blind men who attempt to define an elephant. The first blind man touches the tusk of an elephant and says, "Now I know what the elephant is. It is like a giant carrot." The second blind man touches its ear and declares that it is like a big fan. The third, fourth, and fifth blind men respectively touch its trunk, leg, and tail and declare that it is like a pestle, a mortar, and a rope. These five blind men are firmly convinced that they are absolutely right in their understanding. So they start to fight among themselves.

Then what does it mean to become a "Buddhist"? Here, we must talk about another, sixth, blind man. Then who is the sixth blind man? He is a person who has touched all those five parts of the animal. He is well aware that the elephant has all kinds of parts. He knows that all those five blind men are both right and wrong. He knows that all of them are right, partially right, because they are touching a part of an elephant. But at the same time he knows that all of them are wrong in their view that they have an absolutely correct understanding.

The "Buddhist," the sixth blind man, can identify with all those five blind men, but, at the same time, he cannot agree with them when they say that their own respective views are the only truth. Those five blind men have their fixed positions and they cannot help fighting, whereas the sixth blind man does not have any one position about which he can fight with others. A "Buddhist" is a person who can identify with all human assertions in some way or other, but cannot consider any one assertion the absolute truth.

The most important thing in Buddhism is the realization of a humble attitude, a broad and empty mind, or an all-encompassing mind. This all-embracing spirit is called "Amida Buddha." In the *Larger Sutra*, we read a story in which Dharmakara becomes Amida Buddha. Dharmakara initially vows that he will become a Buddha and create a land where he will encompass all beings. Then, he takes up practices to become a Buddha. His main practice is visiting and worshipping many Buddhas in the ten directions, and studying under them.

The more Buddhas he visits and worships, the humbler he becomes. The humbler he becomes, the more Buddhas he visits and worships. In this way, the number of Buddhas he discovers increases. When he discovers innumerable Buddhas in the ten directions and his whole being becomes worshipping and studying, his Buddhahood is fulfilled. He becomes a Buddha by the name of *Namu Amida Butsu* (Bowing Amida Buddha). Here "Bowing" is part of his Name. In this way Amida Buddha symbolizes the spirit of a perfect student. He has realized an ocean-like mind that can appreciate innumerable Buddhas in the ten directions.

In one verse in his *Hymns of the Pure Land,* Shinran says, "Taking refuge in the Pure Land of Amida means taking refuge in all Buddhas." His words mean the following. Amida Buddha is the all-encompassing spirit itself. When we go to see Amida Buddha in the Pure Land, we just meet the spirit of a perfect student. In his mind we find only innumerable Buddhas whom he is studying and worshipping. We do not find in him even one of his own ideas or thoughts. The contents of his mind are "all Buddhas." Thus Amida is a container of all Buddhas. He encourages us to discover innumerable Buddhas, visit them, and study under them just as he has done himself.

I met my teacher Maida. This does not mean that I have learned a doctrine called "Buddhism" from him. I have not received any fixed idea or thought from him. The only thing I learned from Maida is the spirit of a perfect student. He was nothing but a student and seeker. His humble student spirit has challenged me and deprived me of all the ideas, notions, and opinions that I cherished. I have been reduced to an ignorant student. I have been given a position in which I can appreciate all kinds of teachers and teachings. Maida encourages me to discover "innumerable Buddhas in the ten directions" such as Shakyamuni, Shinran, Shakespeare, Tolstoy, Dostoevsky, Goethe, Gandhi, and Schweitzer, and study under them.

In summary, there are two ways of defining "Buddhism." One is identifying it with a fruit in the basket. The other is identifying it with the basket itself.

If "Buddhism" is a fruit in the basket—a specific doctrine, it is so narrow and limited; it is not true Buddhism. If "Buddhism" is a doctrine that can be compared with other doctrines, that is a misunderstanding of what Shakyamuni taught. If "Buddhism" means such a limited thing, I do not want to become a "Buddhist." I do not want to be called a "Buddhist." But if "Buddhism" means the basket itself, if it means the realization of a broad and empty mind, an ocean-like mind, an all-encompassing mind, I want to become a "Buddhist." If "Buddhist" means a person who can respect all kinds of teachers and study under them, I want to be called a "Buddhist."

Don't become a fruit in the basket! Become the basket! Appreciate all kinds of fruits in the basket! Buddhism is appreciating all kinds of teachers and teachings. There are so many wonderful teachers and teachings in the world. Let's forget labels such as Christianity, Islam, etc. Let's forget even labels such as "Buddhism," "Zen," or "Shin." Let us study from all. We are, after all, all human beings. We share the same human suffering and the same human aspirations. We do not have to be trapped by superficial labels and identities.

# 14

# What Is "Happiness" in Buddhism?

## Introduction

Let me discuss one of the most basic questions in our life, "What is happiness?"

About ten years ago, after a seminar held in a Buddhist temple in Seattle, a university student approached me and said to me, "Dr. Haneda, I am writing a paper on happiness. I am comparing various religious definitions of happiness. Could you give me a Buddhist definition?" I answered, "If you can forget your individual happiness, that's the happiness defined in Buddhism. If the issue of your happiness ceases to be an issue, that's the happiness defined in Buddhism." Then the student asked me, "How, then, can we forget ourselves, our individual happiness?" I answered him, "If you intentionally attempt to forget yourself or your happiness, you will not be able to do so. But if you encounter something more powerful than yourself, something more important than your happiness, then you will be able to forget yourself and your happiness."[70]

From morning to night, we are concerned with our individual welfare, with questions such as what we should eat and wear. Many of us believe that our happiness depends on how successfully we satisfy our personal needs. But is it really the case that our happiness depends on that? No, I do not think so. Actually, the more self-centered we become, the less happy we become.

Generally speaking, who is an unhappy person? An unhappy person is a person who cannot forget himself, being always concerned with his individual happiness and welfare. Probably the Buddhist concept of hell symbolizes the condition in which one has only himself, only his self-concerns such as what he should eat and wear. Then, who is a happy person? A happy person is the person who can forget himself, his individual happiness. He is so fascinated with something outside himself that he can forget himself. A lover is happy because he is thinking of his girlfriend, forgetting himself. An artist is happy because he is absorbed in creative activity, forgetting himself.

## Dōgen's Definition of Buddhism

Now let me further discuss what "happiness" means in Buddhism. The following words of the Zen master Dōgen are probably the best definition of human happiness as well as of Buddhism:

> Studying Buddhism means studying the self. Studying the self means forgetting the self. Forgetting the self means being attained by [the spirit that is one with] tens of thousands of dharmas (things).
>
> —"The *Kōan* of Present Becoming"[71]

The first sentence, "Studying Buddhism means studying the self," clearly defines Buddhism as nothing but self-examination. However, two ways of understanding the first sentence are possible. Depending on which way of understanding we have, we will end up in taking two totally different directions.

First way: When a person is told that Buddhism is a way of self-examination, he thinks that he should focus his attention only on the pursuit of his personal happiness. He thinks that he should be exclusively concerned with the issue of his individual salvation all the time. Thinking this way, he deepens his self-love and self-centeredness.

Second way: When a person is told that Buddhism is a way of self-examination, he focuses his attention on examining the real nature of the self. Then he discovers that the self is nothing worth loving or cherishing. Thinking this way, he becomes less self-attached, less self-centered.

When we start to study Buddhism, it is often inevitable that we take the first way. We initially study Buddhism because we are concerned with the issue of our individual happiness. But Dōgen says that in the course of self-examination, the initial self-centered mentality that seeks individual happiness alone must be transformed. When he says, "Studying the self means forgetting the self," he indicates that true self-examination should end up in discovering the self as something worth forgetting.

The most crucial question is "How can we forget the self?" The answer is that we must meet something powerful and overwhelming. Then, what is powerful and overwhelming in Buddhism? It is the spirit of the bodhisattva. Nothing else can make us forget the self. When Dōgen says, "Forgetting the self means being attained by [the spirit that is one with] tens of thousands of things," he means that the self should meet the spirit of the bodhisattva and be replaced by it. Then, what is the spirit of the bodhisattva? Dōgen defines it as follows:

> Awakening "the spirit of the bodhisattva (*bodhicitta*)" means awakening the aspiration (or vow) that says, "Before I myself cross over to the other shore, I will take all sentient beings across first."
>
> —"Awakening of the *Bodhicitta*"[72]

The bodhisattva spirit is the spirit that is concerned with the happiness of all sentient beings, forgetting one's own happiness. This self-forgetting spirit of the bodhisattva is powerful. Only when we meet this spirit and become overwhelmed and permeated by it can we forget ourselves, our own happiness. We usually do not think it possible to identify with such a noble spirit. But, when we *actually meet* a person who possesses the powerful bodhisattva spirit and become overwhelmed by it, we can experience a spiritual transformation and forget the self.

So long as we seek our own happiness, we will never be able to attain it. But when we meet the bodhisattva spirit, we can forget our own happiness. This self-forgetfulness, however, is actually the experience of our true happiness. This true happiness (or self-forgetfulness) is nothing that we can actively realize or "attain." It is something that is realized from the side of the Buddha or Dharma, without any recourse to our own practical abilities. That is why Dōgen uses the word "attained" in his statement, "Forgetting the self means being attained by [the spirit that is one with] tens of thousands of things."

Now let me discuss the same issue within the context of Shin Buddhism. The bodhisattva spirit (that aspires to take all sentient beings across first before doing so oneself) is the spiritual basis of the bodhisattva Dharmakara and of his vows that he made to become Amida Buddha. If I summarize in one sentence the gist of Dharmakara's vows, he is saying, "If all sentient beings are not liberated, I will not attain liberation." Here he is expressing his aspiration to "take all sentient beings across first before doing so himself."

Dharmakara is not concerned with his own individual liberation. He is concerned with the liberation of all sentient beings, forgetting his own liberation. But his being concerned with all sentient beings' liberation is actually his liberation. Being able to forget his own liberation is itself his liberation.

### Ajatasatru's Encounter with Shakyamuni's Compassion

Now let me talk about King Ajatasatru. Shinran identified himself with this king. The famous story of King Ajatasatru is told in the *Nirvana Sutra*.[73]

King Ajatasatru is a historical example of the most evil person (*icchantika*). When he was a prince, he killed his father, the king, and usurped his throne. Further, he attempted to kill his mother. Although he did not kill her, he imprisoned her. But later he started to feel tremendous remorse for having committed such hideous transgressions.

Several spiritual teachers attempted to console Ajatasatru, but his spiritual sickness was not cured. Finally, when Jivaka, a Buddhist physician, advised the king to visit Shakyamuni, he decided to do so. When the king and Jivaka started to travel, the king asked Jivaka to ride on the same elephant because he feared that he might fall off the elephant, die, and go to hell. The king said to Jivaka, "Please hold me and keep me from falling. For I have heard in the past that the person who has attained the way does not fall into hell."

While the king was traveling to see Shakyamuni, he learned of Shakyamuni's words, "For the sake of Ajatasatru, I will not enter nirvana." Jivaka told the king that although Shakyamuni was concerned with the welfare of all sentient beings, he was particularly concerned with people like Ajatasatru, who have committed evil.

Having learned about the compassionate heart of Shakyamuni, the king was deeply moved. Having recognized the remarkable contrast between Shakyamuni's mind (that was concerned with the welfare of suffering sentient beings) and his own mind (that was concerned only with his personal welfare), the king became ashamed of himself. When the king met Shakyamuni, he received teachings from him and experienced liberation. The king then awakened the bodhisattva spirit. He came up with an extraordinary statement, "World-honored one, if I can thoroughly destroy the evil minds of sentient beings, it is all right with me if I dwell in the Avici hell constantly for innumerable *kalpa*s, undergoing great suffering for the sake of sentient beings. I would not consider it pain."

Initially, when the king was concerned only with his individual welfare, he was afraid of falling into hell. But now when he had awakened the bodhisattva spirit, he was concerned with the welfare of all sentient beings, forgetting his own welfare. Now he said that he would willingly go to hell if he could help sentient beings.

The king compares his old self to an *eranda* tree, a tree with the worst odor, and his new *shinjin* self to a *candana* tree, a tree with the most exquisite fragrance. He said, "Now for the first time I see a *candana* tree growing from an *eranda* seed." In this way, the king describes the spiritual miracle that he has experienced, having met Shakyamuni.

## Shinran's Encounter with Dharmakara's Compassion

Now let me talk about Shinran. For twenty years, from age eight to twenty-eight, Shinran engaged in various practices on Mt. Hiei in an attempt to attain Buddhahood. But those practices did not lead him to Buddhahood. Not only was he unable to become a Buddha, but he was also feeling more and more depressed, frustrated, and miserable as he intensified his practices. He could not understand what was wrong.

When Shinran was twenty-eight, he met Hōnen. It was through this meeting that Shinran was liberated. When Shinran met Hōnen, he saw in him the bodhisattva spirit of Dharmakara. Hōnen was permeated with the bodhisattva spirit. He was concerned with the happiness of all sentient beings, forgetting his own happiness. I believe that Hōnen's spirit, the self-forgetting spirit, shouted at Shinran this way:

> Shinran, what are you doing? You say that you are seeking Buddhahood. But, after all, aren't you thinking only about your individual happiness? Aren't you concerned only with your individual liberation? You are dead wrong in your approach. You are just using Buddhism for self-enhancement, for self-love.

Listening to the voice of Hōnen, Shinran was deeply shaken by it and recognized his mistake. He realized that he was no different from Ajatasatru. Just like the king who saw the bodhisattva spirit in Shakyamuni and became ashamed of his self-centeredness, Shinran saw the bodhisattva spirit in Hōnen and became ashamed of his self-centeredness.

Before Shinran met Hōnen, Shinran lived in a world of self-love, but he did not know it. Hōnen's spirit of the bodhisattva challenged Shinran and made a crack in his world of self-love. Then cool fresh air started to gush into his world. When Shinran experienced the cool fresh air gushing into his world, he realized that he had been living in a world of self-love.

Hōnen's spirit, the cool fresh air, made Shinran recognize that he had been living in "a garbage can" and that the entirety of the self had been nothing but "a garbage can." He had earlier believed that he could find something pure and fragrant in the garbage can and could increase its purity and fragrance. But now he recognized it was a mistake. He realized that there was only stinkiness in the garbage can. Even what he considered purity in it was another form of stinkiness.

Thus Shinran no longer considered the self, the garbage can, important. Now he considered the self worth forgetting. Being overwhelmed and permeated by Hōnen's spirit, the fresh air, Shinran shifted his focus from the self to the spirit that Hōnen embodied, from the garbage can to the fresh air. In this way Shinran's spiritual basis was totally changed.

Shinran called the spirit of Dharmakara that he saw in Hōnen "Innermost Aspiration." Shinran considered the power of the Innermost Aspiration the most important thing in Buddhism. He believed that it alone could bring about spiritual revolution in human beings and could make them fulfill their lives. He also referred to this power as the Power Beyond the Self (*ta-riki*) and the Inconceivable Power (*fukashigi-riki*). Since this power is the basic theme of the *Larger Sutra,* he considered this *sutra* the most important text for him.

## Conclusion

Initially, when we are told that Buddhism is a way of self-examination, of self-focusedness, we think that we should pursue our personal liberation. Thus we engage in various practices. Many people continue this orientation throughout their lives and never recognize the deep self-love that exists at the basis of their practices.

But Buddhist teachers tell us that a radical transformation of our spiritual basis must take place. We must know that our ultimate liberation is not realized through the efforts we make on the basis of self-love. True liberation is nothing we can "attain." It is realized and "attained" from the side of the Buddha, or the Dharma. We must experience a total transformation of our spiritual basis by encountering the spirit of the bodhisattva.

As long as the power of the Innermost Aspiration remains a mere doctrinal concept, it does not mean much to us; we cannot experience any deep spiritual transformation. But if we, like Ajatasatru or Shinran, *actually meet* a person who has the power of the Innermost

Aspiration, a spiritual revolution that our ego-consciousness would never have considered possible takes place. When we are shaken and overwhelmed by this power, we resonate with it and can forget our individual happiness or liberation. This self-forgetfulness is actually the realization of our true happiness or liberation.

# 15

# Specificity

## Introduction

In this essay I want to emphasize the importance of having a specific orientation in Buddhism. I believe that it is important and necessary to belong to a specific tradition, to study under a specific teacher, and to study specific texts. When we read the biographies of our eminent Buddhist predecessors such as Shinran and Dōgen, we learn that all of them had very specific orientations.

One of the most outstanding features of Shin Buddhism is that it emphasizes the importance of taking a specific path toward the universal truth. However, many Buddhists whom we might call "Buddhist universalists" consider the Shin Buddhist way a narrow, one-sided, and misguided one. In this essay I want to say that this universalist criticism of Shin Buddhism is not valid and that if we are serious about realizing the universal truth, it is crucially important that we take a specific way.

## Shinran's Specific Orientation

First, let me talk about Shinran's specific orientation by quoting his words as recorded in the second chapter of the *Tannishō*:

> Each one of you has come to see me, having crossed the boundaries of more than ten provinces at the risk of your lives. The sole purpose of your trip here is that you wish to hear from me the way to be born in the Realm of Utmost Happiness.
>
> If, however, you think that I know of ways to attain birth other than the *nembutsu* [i.e., appreciation of the meaning contained in Amida's name], or that I know some secret

131

scriptures, you are greatly mistaken. If you think so, you had better visit the many distinguished scholars in Nara and on Mt. Hiei and ask them questions concerning the essentials for birth.

As far as I, Shinran, am concerned, I just receive and entrust myself to the words of the good person [i.e., Hōnen], "Be liberated by Amida by saying the *nembutsu.*" That's all.[74]

Here we can see Shinran contrasting two Buddhist ways, the general (or academic) way that is represented by the scholars of Nara and Mt. Hiei, and Shinran's own specific way. Shinran tells his visitors that if they are interested in knowing the Dharma in a general way, they had better leave him and visit scholars. Then he describes his own way. He says that he is concerned with birth in the Realm of Utmost Happiness, one specific land, and Amida Buddha, one specific Buddha. He says that he has one specific teacher, Hōnen, and is receiving one specific teaching from him. He also says that he honors the *nembutsu,* one specific practice. Further, at the beginning of his *Kyōgyōshinshō,* Shinran indicates that all of his Buddhist ideas are based on the *Larger Sutra,* one specific text, a text that reveals the ultimate truth. In this way, we can see that concerning all aspects of his Buddhism, Shinran was very specific.

### Universalists' Criticism of Shinran's Specific Way

Shinran represented the Pure Land tradition. However, throughout Buddhist history in China and Japan, many Buddhist universalist scholars criticized the specific orientation of the Pure Land tradition and the Pure Land masters such as Shan-tao, Hōnen, and Shinran, claiming, "Buddhism teaches us the universal truth. It teaches us that there are many wonderful Buddhas, Buddha-lands, teachers, teachings, and texts. We should appreciate them all equally. Thus selecting one teacher, one teaching, or one text and honoring it is too narrow an approach. It is a kind of prejudice or dogmatism."

These words of Buddhist universalists sounded plausible and many people agreed with them. It was this universalist criticism of the Pure Land tradition that was the basis of the persecution of teachers such as Hōnen and Shinran. It was "the scholars in Nara and on Mt. Hiei" who asked the government to persecute them.

Then, how does Shinran respond to the challenge of Buddhist universalists? I believe Shinran would answer in this way: "Yes, you are right in saying that Buddhism teaches the Dharma, the universal truth. The Dharma is the most important thing in Buddhism. My advocacy of a specific way does not mean that I am neglecting the universal truth. On the contrary, I am concerned with *a realistic way* of attaining it. It is only through a specific channel that I can reach the universal truth."

To explain this view of Shinran, let me give the following example. Suppose all of us are interested in watching the stars in the sky. Then, the first thing we each have to do is get a telescope. When we get our telescopes, we look into them and see the stars in the sky.

Here two things are involved: a telescope and stars. First, we get telescopes that are specifically for us. We cannot share our respective telescopes with others; two people cannot look into the same telescope at the same time. Then, how about the stars that we see through our telescopes? Are they specific too? No. Although our telescopes are specific, the stars that we see are not specific. They are universal; we all see the same stars. Looking through specific telescopes does not mean that we see different stars in the sky. The same thing can be said about our appreciation of the Dharma, the universal truth. We must first have a specific channel. It is only through this specific channel that we can reach the universal truth.

## Taking a Ferryboat to the Other Shore

To further explain the importance of taking a specific way, let me talk about another example. I also want to point out a danger contained in taking a specific way.

Buddhism is traditionally said to have eighty-four thousand Dharma gates (or teachings). The eighty-four thousand Dharma gates are often compared to "ferryboats" that carry people from this shore (i.e., the world of suffering) to the other shore (i.e., the world of awakening).

Suppose Mr. A is traveling and on the way he encounters a lion. Being chased by the beast, Mr. A desperately runs away from it and comes to a river where he discovers many ferryboats stationed on this side. He immediately gets on a ferryboat and starts to cross the river to the other shore. Mr. B happens to be there by the river. He looks at what Mr. A is doing and starts to laugh at him. Mr. B says, "What a narrow-minded thing Mr. A is doing! He is using only one boat. All these ferryboats are wonderful. We should appreciate them all equally. It is not right to choose one boat."

To me Shinran is like Mr. A and Buddhist universalists are like Mr. B. The main difference between them is that Mr. A sees the lion and is desperately running away from it, whereas, Mr. B is not aware of the terrible beast. The ferryboats have totally different meanings to these two individuals. For Mr. A a ferryboat is something he has to use immediately as a means of rescue, of going to the other shore. He is so desperate that he immediately gets on it; he has no time to examine or admire various boats. For Mr. B, ferryboats are objects to examine or admire. He is objectively and leisurely watching them *on this shore*. If he became aware of the lion that is coming to attack him, he would certainly do the same thing that Mr. A is doing. But unfortunately he cannot see the lion.

Here I cannot help talking about the scholars who are engaged in the comparative study of religions. Many of them say that they are objective and do not belong to any one religious tradition, and that they see all teachings objectively and impartially. But I must say that they do not have any insight into "the lion" and do not feel any need to run away from it. Scholars of comparative religion are not traveling to the other shore, because in order to make a comparative study of various teachings (ferryboats), they must be standing *on this shore*. Comparing various ferryboats is possible only when a person is standing *on this shore*. If we are serious about going to the other shore, we cannot possibly have the leisure to make a comparative study. We will immediately get on a boat and leave this shore. Realistically speaking, one ferryboat is all we need. We don't need two or more boats.

But there is one danger that we must bear in mind: a ferryboat is only a means by which we go to the other shore. Reaching the other shore is the most important thing. Although we all must have our own specific ferryboats, the other shore that we reach is the same for everyone; it is the universal truth. The ferryboat is not something to which we should become attached. If we become attached to it and forget about going to the other shore, we will never get to the other shore. Then, universalists' criticism of the specific way is quite valid.

Thus concerning our travel to the other shore, we should know that there are two *must*s. The first *must* is that we *must* have a ferryboat to go to the other shore. The second *must* is that when we have reached the other shore, we *must* leave the ferryboat. We *must* say "Good-bye" to it.

We must have a specific channel (a specific teacher or teaching) to reach the universal truth. But when we reach the universal truth, our focus should be placed on it alone; we should not be attached to the channel.

## T'an-luan and a Buddhist Emperor

There is a famous story about T'an-luan:

T'an-luan lived during the Liang dynasty in North China. The emperor of this dynasty was a Buddhist scholar who was well versed in all kinds of Buddhist doctrines. One day this Buddhist emperor was informed that there was an eminent monk by the name of T'an-luan. He also learned that T'an-luan performed Pure Land practices; he worshipped Amida Buddha and chanted the Buddha's Name. Being a widely read scholar, the emperor thought that T'an-luan's approach was very narrow. He thought he should visit and challenge the Pure Land master. When the emperor visited T'an-luan at his temple, he said to the teacher, "O, Dharma master, I have been studying Buddhism. I have learned that there are innumerable Buddhas and innumerable Buddha-lands in the ten directions.

O, Dharma master, why do you direct your attention exclusively to Amida Buddha, one Buddha, and to Amida's Pure Land, one Buddha-land? Is this not some kind of narrowness or prejudice?" To this T'an-luan replied, "Your imperial majesty, I am a foolish ordinary person. My wisdom is shallow and limited. I have not yet attained a high rank in Buddhism. If I were a superior practitioner, I might be able to concentrate my mind everywhere and see Pure Lands everywhere. But my mind is restless and lacks concentration. How can I concentrate my mind without having one specific object? So for me, focusing on Amida Buddha is like putting hay in front of a foolish donkey. Since the donkey's mind is always concentrated on the manger, how could it lose its concentration?" When the emperor listened to these words, he was deeply moved by the humility that T'an-luan manifested.

Initially the emperor thought that T'an-luan was an arrogant person because he seemed to be attached to one Buddha. But now the emperor realized that T'an-luan's approach was based on his humble self-understanding—on his insight into his foolishness. Now the emperor realized that T'an-luan was a humble person and that he himself was an arrogant person who had a shallow understanding of Buddhism. He recognized his mistake of identifying with a higher stage in Buddhism without experiencing the crucial first step of knowing his own foolishness and without having a specific way because of his foolishness.

This story tells us that objectively and generally knowing about the universal truth is one thing; it is quite another to appreciate it subjectively and experientially in a specific context. True Buddhism exists in the latter.

## Conclusion

I have discussed the importance of taking a specific way, which is one of the most outstanding doctrinal features of Shin Buddhist. Although the specific way is often criticized by Buddhist universalists, I believe it is the realistic way of attaining the universal truth. We must take a specific way; we must have specific teachers and texts to learn from.

The more desperate we become, the more specific we become in our approach. We are not angels; we are not living in the world of abstract ideas. We are all specific human beings; we have specific karmic experiences and backgrounds. It is only through a specific way that we can get to the universal truth. Buddhism is a teaching in which we see universality in specificity. It is not a teaching in which we see universality in universality. Rev. Haya Akegarasu said:

> Both those who have many teachers and those who have
>     no teacher have not yet discovered their own way.
> Both those who worship many gods and Buddhas and
>     those who worship no god and no Buddha have not yet
>     discovered the world of truth.
> Blessed are those who have only one teacher, who serve
>     only one Buddha![75]

# 16

# Universality

## Introduction

What is the universal truth that can make us one? This question is particularly important in the United States where we have cultural and religious diversity that is hardly matched by other countries in the world.

Major religions of the world consist of two types of components: specific (cultural, doctrinal, etc.) components and universal components. As far as specific components are concerned, we respect each others' different customs, rituals, and practices. Here diversity is beauty. But it is not good enough to respect each other's specific cultural and doctrinal orientations; we must go beyond them and identify the universal truth, the one common denominator, which can make all people one.

A common mistake is to become attached to our own specific orientation and not pay attention to the universal truth. Or, we may mistake our own specific ethno-culturally oriented teachings for the universal truth. It is so important for us to remember that it is not a specific teaching but the universal truth that is the core of religion.

I would compare specific religious components to containers and the universal truth to water. We honor various containers because without them the water simply cannot exist. We honor their uniqueness. There is nothing wrong with loving and appreciating our respective containers. But we have to bear in mind that it is not the container but the water that quenches our thirst and gives us life.

Many advocates of religions are attached to their own specific teachings. It is ironic that what they call the universal truth divides people and creates conflicts and fights. Why do they have to fight if they are taking refuge in the universal truth, one truth? Shouldn't the universal truth make them become one?

Thus it is crucially important to ask, "What is the universal truth that can make us become one?" In this essay I want to answer this question by discussing the Dharma, the universal truth, which is taught in Shin Buddhism.

## The Universal Truth Taught in Shin Buddhism

Shinran was specific in every aspect of his life as a Buddhist. For example, he was a follower of a tradition called Pure Land Buddhism that talks about Amida Buddha, one Buddha, as the basis of human liberation. Shinran had a personal teacher by the name of Hōnen. He was grateful to him for guiding him to other Pure Land masters and their teachings. Shinran also honored one text, the *Larger Sutra*, as the text that reveals the ultimate truth.

However, Shinran was not attached to Pure Land teachers and their teachings. He honored them because they guided him to the universal truth. For Shinran, those teachers and teachings were like a telescope that enabled him to see stars or a pipeline that enabled him to receive life-giving water.

What, then, is the universal truth that Shinran appreciated? It is the Innermost Aspiration to seek truth continuously. Let me explain what the Innermost Aspiration means by discussing the contents of the *Larger Sutra*. This text explains the concept with the story of Dharmakara (or Amida), a symbol of the perpetual seeker.

Dharmakara meets a Buddha. Having been deeply moved by the Buddha's spirit, Dharmakara generates the aspiration to become a Buddha like him and to create a wonderful Buddha-land. Thus he requests teachings. The Buddha instructs him on the importance of endless seeking and learning, and shows him innumerable Buddha-lands that exist in the ten directions. This way, the Buddha teaches the seeker that the most important thing for him to do is to learn endlessly from innumerable Buddhas. Having received the teacher's instructions, Dharmakara expresses his Innermost Aspiration in words (vows) and takes up his practices to realize it. His main practice is visiting innumerable Buddhas in the ten directions and learning from them. And eventually, after a long period of practice, he becomes a Buddha by the name of Amida Buddha and creates the Pure Land, a place to which he welcomes all sentient beings. As soon as they are born there, they become perpetual seekers and are promised eventual attainment of Buddhahood.

We can see the basic nature of Dharmakara's Innermost Aspiration and his practice in the following words of the "Verses in Praise of a Buddha":

Even though there are zillions of Buddhas
And great sages as many as the sand grains of the
    River Ganges,
I will visit all of them and study under them.
Nothing is greater than seeking the way, continuously
    advancing and never retreating.

Even though the Buddha countries are as innumerable
    as the sand grains of the River Ganges,
And other lands are also without number,
My light will illuminate all those countries and lands,
    spreading all over them.
Such will be the way I will make continuous efforts,
    and my power will be limitless.

Visiting Buddhas as many as the sand grains of the River Ganges and studying under them is Dharmakara's main practice. Through this practice he aspires to realize limitless light, limitless wisdom.

I believe that this Innermost Aspiration, the aspiration to learn endlessly from innumerable Buddhas, is "the universal truth" that Shin Buddhism teaches.

Let me explain this Aspiration of Dharmakara with an illustration. Suppose there is a huge basket that contains innumerable fruits such as apples, oranges, and pears. I could compare Dharmakara's Aspiration to the basket and the innumerable Buddhas in the ten directions to the innumerable fruits that are contained in it. In his practice, Dharmakara is not aspiring to become one specific fruit in the basket. He is not satisfied with possessing a fixed doctrine or dogma. He is aspiring to become a basket that can encompass a limitless number of fruits. He is aspiring to develop a mind that can encompass a limitless number of Buddhas and appreciate their teachings. He is aspiring to become a perfect seeker and deepen the process of seeking and learning.

The *Larger Sutra* says that through his practice of visiting Buddhas, Dharmakara eventually perfects his seeker's spirit. Thus, his name becomes Amitabha (limitless light). This Name means that he has realized the spirit that endlessly seeks "light" (wisdom). This Innermost Aspiration, this ever-seeking spirit, is "the universal truth" that Shin Buddhism teaches. It is not a fixed position, not a fixed dogma or doctrine. It is the dynamic seeking process itself.

If we have a fixed position, we will become a fruit in the basket and start to compare ourselves with the other fruits. Since all the fruits in the basket like to feel superior to the others, it is inevitable that they will start to fight among themselves. But the Innermost Aspiration is the spirit that aspires to embrace all fruits. It cannot be compared with the fruits in the basket.

## Historical Manifestations of the Universal Truth

Now I have said that the Innermost Aspiration (that Dharmakara symbolizes) is the universal truth taught in Shin Buddhism. Then how did the universal truth appear in Buddhist history? Let me talk about three individuals, Shakyamuni, Shinran, and Rev. Manshi Kiyozawa, all of whom received the Innermost Aspiration from their predecessors. Their experiences can be called the *shinjin* experience — awakening realized through the Power Beyond the Self. They recognized the emptiness of the self, and were filled with the Innermost Aspiration. Having become embodiers of the Aspiration, they all lived their lives as dynamic seekers.

After encountering a traveling monk and having the aspiration for Buddhahood awakened by him, Shakyamuni left his householder's life and became a seeker of the path. He visited and learned from various spiritual teachers of his time. After having thoroughly learned what those teachers could teach him, he sat under a tree and meditated. In this meditation he attained enlightenment. He understood that everything was impermanent and there was nothing fixed or permanent in the self. Thus he recognized the emptiness of the self (which is called selflessness). However the recognition of subjective emptiness was the realization of his dynamic life. He discovered that the essence of his being was the Dharma, dynamic seeking itself. Being a continuous seeker and learner became his whole life.

Shakyamuni realized the spiritual realm that transcended any fixed position, relativity, and comparison. He said:

> The person who views things as equal, better, or worse from his comparative perspective will always argue with others. But the person who does not take up the three comparative ideas will not view things as equal, better, or worse. Pointing to what does the attainer of the path assert, "This is truth"? Toward whom does he argue, "That is false"? With whom does the person who has ceased to say "equal" or "not equal" start to argue?
>
> —*Sutta-nipata*, No. 843[76]

Here Shakyamuni is talking about the Innermost Aspiration—the ever-seeking and all-encompassing spirit that transcends relativity. Throughout his life Shakyamuni kept on seeking and learning. He was never satisfied with possessing any fixed position or viewpoint. The famous last message he left immediately before his death was "Disciples, make continuous effort in seeking and learning."[77]

Shinran met Hōnen, who embodied the Innermost Aspiration, the spirit of a perpetual seeker. In spite of the fact that people of his time called Hōnen a man of wisdom, Hōnen called himself a foolish person and kept on humbly seeking the Dharma from his predecessors. Having witnessed the Innermost Aspiration in Hōnen, Shinran recognized the total evilness and ignorance of his being. This was his experience of subjective emptiness or nothingness, which was simultaneously the experience of being permeated by the power of the Innermost Aspiration. Thus Shinran started to live as a constant seeker. He said, "I, Shinran, do not have even one single disciple." Throughout his life he never identified himself as a teacher but lived the life of a humble student.

Shinran's tradition is known as Shin Buddhism (*shinshū*). The term *shinshū* and the term *hongan* (the Innermost Aspiration) were synonymous in Shinran's mind. The term *shinshū* means "true religion" or "universal religion"; it refers to *hongan*, the aspiration to learn from everybody and everything. In Shinran's mind, the term *shinshū* did not have any sectarian connotation.

Shinran said, "The way of the Innermost Aspiration is outside the 84,000 Buddhist teachings."[78] Here Shinran is saying the same thing I said earlier in the metaphor about fruits and a basket. He is saying that the Innermost Aspiration is not one of the 84,000 fruits in the basket and that it cannot be compared with the other 83,999 fruits. He is saying that the Innermost Aspiration is an all-encompassing basket—that it is the basis of all the fruits and underlies all of them. The Innermost Aspiration is the spirit that desires to learn from all 84,000 fruits without becoming one of them.

Having been permeated by this Innermost Aspiration, Shinran lived the life of a humble seeker. He kept on appreciating all kinds of teachers and teachings.

In modern times, we have Rev. Manshi Kiyozawa. After intense examination of the basic nature of the self, Rev. Kiyozawa recognized its emptiness. He expressed this insight in his pen name "December Fan,"[79] that means a totally useless thing. However, this realization of subjective emptiness was the realization of the dynamic process of seeking in his being—the realization of the Innermost Aspiration.

Concerning Kiyozawa, Rev. Haya Akegarasu, his student, said:

> During the three years that I lived with my teacher Rev. Kiyozawa at the Kōkōdō dormitory in Tokyo, he never once accepted anything I said. Suppose that today I asserted something; then Rev. Kiyozawa completely destroyed my logic. The next day I would agree with what he said the day before and repeat his words; but he would completely destroy that too. The following day, after trying to figure out

his meaning, I would make another assertion; and he would crush me completely again.[80]

Akegarasu's words sound as if Kiyozawa were a nihilist or an arrogant teacher who loved to negate his students. But he was not so much a nihilist or an arrogant teacher as he was a humble seeker of the Dharma. Kiyozawa was an embodiment of the Innermost Aspiration, the spirit of the constant seeker. He was not content with any fixed ideas or positions and was always seeking and learning. His ever-seeking spirit could not help becoming a challenging force for his students, such as Akegarasu.

## Conclusion

If we think that Shin Buddhism is a sectarian teaching that can be compared with other teachings and found to be superior to them, we totally misunderstand Shin Buddhism. Such Shin is just another fruit that can be compared with other fruits in the basket. It is not the Shin Buddhism that Shinran taught.

Shin Buddhism, the way of the Innermost Aspiration, is the process of humble and dynamic seeking itself. It cannot be compared with other fruits in the basket. The most important thing is that we realize subjective emptiness (or nothingness) and become humble seekers who can learn from all kinds of teachers and teachings.

If we are attached to a fixed position, then although we may consider it universal, it cannot be the universal principle that can make us one. Only the humble spirit that keeps on learning from everyone and everything can be the universal principle that can make us one. It is only when we all become humble seekers and learn from each other that we can become one.

I think it important to know that the essence of Shin Buddhism transcends what we commonly know as "Buddhism." That is what Shinran meant when he said, "The way of the Innermost Aspiration is outside the 84,000 Buddhist teachings." It is this universal truth, this universal spirit, that Shinran appreciated in the specific tradition called Pure Land Buddhism and that we must identify at the core of our respective religious traditions.

# 17

# "Put Your Lips to the Dust!"

## Introduction

In this essay I want to talk about the similarity between the religious experiences of a modern Japanese Christian and those of a Buddhist. More specifically, I want to talk about the similarity between the religious experiences of Mr. Hideo Nishimura, a contemporary Japanese Christian, and those of Shinran.

We often talk about the differences between Christianity and Buddhism. It is easy for us to discuss the theoretical or doctrinal differences between the two religions, but it is not easy to talk about their differences as far as the actual experiences of Christians and Buddhists are concerned. After all, we are all the same human beings; we share the same human suffering and the same aspiration to be liberated from it. We must have deep respect for all people who are suffering and trying to find a way out of suffering, regardless of their different religious orientations.

## Mr. Hideo Nishimura

Now let me talk about Mr. Hideo Nishimura, a Christian. I had never heard his name before a friend in Japan recently sent me a videotape containing a TV program about his life. In this program an interviewer asked Mr. Nishimura all kinds of questions.

Mr. Nishimura was born in 1919 and is now eighty-seven years old. He is not a famous spiritual leader or scholar. He is an ordinary Christian social worker who is working with the mentally and physically disabled.

When Mr. Nishimura was a student at Tokyo University, he met Professor Tadao Yanaihara (1893–1961, a famous Christian educator). Mr. Nishimura was so deeply impressed by this professor that he became a Christian. After graduating from the university, he served in the Japanese army in Manchuria. When Japan was defeated in the Second World War, he came back to Japan and became a professor at Tokyo University.

In the TV program about his life, Mr. Nishimura talked about the statements of three individuals that deeply struck him and eventually transformed his life. Let me talk about those three statements. The first statement that hit him deeply came from his second son.

In the late 1960's when Mr. Nishimura was around fifty, it was the peak of the students' movement in Japan. Actually many students all over the world were protesting the United States' involvement in the Vietnam War. At that time Mr. Nishimura was working as a student advisor in the department of students' affairs at Tokyo University. He was playing a difficult role as a negotiator between radical students and the school administration. Radical students were constantly fighting with the police. It was a very bloody time.

On one of those turbulent days, Mr. Nishimura had a conversation with his second son, who was participating in the student movement and was struggling to find meaning in his life. At one point in their conversation, the son said, "Dad, speak to me! Come down to me! Dad, you are speaking in such an abstract and condescending way!"

Mr. Nishimura said to the interviewer that he knew that his son was seriously searching for meaning in his life. But he was not able to recognize the weight of his son's words when he said, "Dad, speak to me! Come down to me!" Mr. Nishimura thought he was familiar with the psychology of young students because he was an advisor in the department of students' affairs at a university.

The next day, the son committed suicide. Mr. Nishimura was devastated. Having experienced the death of his own son, he realized that he had not understood the young man at all and was not standing on the same level with him. He realized that he had been assuming the position of teacher and advisor to his son; he had been preaching down to him. Now Mr. Nishimura recognized the importance of his son's words "Dad, speak to me! Come down to me! Dad, you are speaking in such an abstract and condescending way!" Those words were deeply ingrained in his mind.

Now let me talk about the second statement that hit Mr. Nishimura deeply. It was the words of an ancient prophet in the Old Testament. When Mr. Nishimura was suffering from the loss of his son, he received a letter from one of his Christian friends. In that letter, his friend, sympathizing with him, quoted the words of the prophet in the Old Testament. The words were, "Put your lips to the dust and you will have hope."[81] This was about the importance of coming down from a high position, an arrogant spiritual position, and the importance of going down to reality, of identifying oneself with the nitty-gritty basis of human existence. Mr. Nishimura felt that these words contained a deep message for him.

Now let me talk about the third statement that shook Mr. Nishimura. After his son's death, both he and his wife started to suffer from severe cases of depression. They both began to receive psychiatric treatment. Some time later, Mr. and Mrs. Nishimura were both placed in a treatment center. The center was a two-story building; the first floor was for female patients and the second floor was for male patients. Mrs. Nishimura lived on the first floor and Mr. Nishimura lived on the second floor. These two floors were separated and male patients and female patients were not supposed to associate with each other.

One day Mr. Nishimura went down to the first floor to give a message to his wife, who was on the first floor. While he was on the first floor visiting his wife, a nurse discovered that he was there. Not knowing that he was visiting his wife, the nurse got quite upset and shouted, "Mister, what the hell are you doing here?" She scolded him as if he were a small child breaking a rule.

Concerning this experience Mr. Nishimura said to his interviewer, "When the nurse shouted at me, I dropped down. I fell down. I was totally grounded. And it was a tremendous relief." When he said so, his interviewer was quite puzzled and asked him, "Mr. Nishimura, what do you mean by saying that you dropped down and that you were totally grounded? And it was a tremendous relief?"

Then Mr. Nishimura answered, "When the nurse scolded me, she was seeing me only as a mental patient. She was treating me only as a mental patient who was breaking a rule. Initially I felt anger toward her. But I immediately realized that she was right. Yes, I was nothing but that. I was nothing but a mental patient. Up to that time I had pride as a teacher, as an academic advisor. But she was seeing me as a mental patient. Yes, that was precisely what I was. When I recognized what I really was, I felt that all of my heavy load was taken off from my shoulders and I experienced tremendous relief. I became what I really was."

When Mr. Nishimura left the treatment center and returned to normal life, he resigned his post as a professor at Tokyo University and started to work with the mentally and physically disabled.

## Mr. Nishimura and Shinran

In the interview program Mr. Nishimura talked about the three statements that hit him. The first was his son's statement "Dad, come down to me!" The second was an ancient prophet's statement "Put your lips to the dust, and you will have hope." And the third statement was "Mister, what the hell are you doing here?"

In these three statements I can see the deepening process of Mr. Nishimura's self-understanding and awakening. I can see him dropping down and settling down into his reality, into what he really was. Those three statements were telling him to come down from the height of his spiritual arrogance and of his self-perception as a teacher, as a spiritually superior person. When the nurse scolded him, he was grounded in reality. Up to that time he thought that he was a teacher. But his pride as a teacher was totally crushed by her words. This crushing of his pride as a good and worthy person was a relief for him.

Mr. Nishimura's experience reminds me of the experience of Shinran. I cannot help thinking of Shinran's famous words in the *Tannishō*: "Even a good person can be born in the Pure Land, how much more so an evil person!"[82]

150

What is a good person here? A good person is a person who thinks himself worthy and important. What is an evil person? An evil person is a person who has transcended his sense of self-worth and self-importance. He has fallen from a spiritual height. He is a person who "is putting his lips to the dust"—who is one with the dust, and is grounded. When Shinran said, "How much more so an evil person!" he was saying that a person who has hit the dust and transcended his sense of self-worth and self-importance can experience tremendous spiritual relief.

I also recollect Shinran's words, "Since I am incapable of performing any religious practice, hell is my only home." Shinran had this realization when he met his teacher Hōnen. Hōnen challenged Shinran, and Shinran started to realize that he was a totally evil and foolish being.

When Shinran said those words, he was deeply grounded in the karmic evil of human nature. He was seeing in himself all kinds of human evil, defects, and shortcomings. He was identifying himself with the deepest dust, the bottom dust, of human existence. However, this experience was simultaneously tremendous liberation for him. He was experiencing a tremendous liberation from his sense of self-importance. He was liberated into a world where he could be one with all humanity.

Shinran had the "grounding" experience not only when he met Hōnen who challenged him, but also when he was exiled to Echigo, a snow country. It was in Echigo that he was awakened to the equality of all humanity. He clearly saw that all human beings were the same—that all human beings were foolish ordinary beings. He said, "We are all weed-like beings" or "We are like stones and pebbles."[83] By these words he meant that all people were ordinary beings and nobody was special.

Here let me talk about Rev. Manshi Kiyozawa. Rev. Kiyozawa also saw himself as a person who has fallen down to the ground and hit the dust. He described himself with the Japanese term "*raku-zai*"[84] which means, "I have dropped down and settled down at the bottom." All his self-importance and wonderful self-perception were shattered by the teachings of his predecessors and various difficult experiences in his life. He says in one of his essays:

> Both our anguish and grief exist because of our sense of self-importance. If we have already lost our sense of self-importance, we do not feel anguish and grief. If we have already lost it, we do not mind whether others despise or honor us, or whether they slight or respect us. We can do all things calmly, leaving others to respect or despise us as they like.[85]

## Conclusion

I have talked about the similarity that I see between the experience of Mr. Nishimura, a Christian, and the experience of Shinran, a Buddhist. Although we could use the label of Christian experience to describe Mr. Nishimura's experience and the label of Buddhist experience to describe Shinran's experience, these two types of experience are basically no different. Both experienced the same spiritual awakening and liberation. They each became an evil person, a person who does not see any importance in his self. When Mr. Nishimura and Shinran recognized the emptiness or meaninglessness of the self that they had cherished, they both were born into a tremendous world of liberation.

# 18

# The Happiness
# the Handless Hand Received

## Introduction

There are two ways of seeing the self. One is seeing it as something independent and autonomous; and the other is seeing it as interdependent and interconnected with all things and people that exist outside it. Here I want to discuss this issue by referring to an experience that Rev. Junkyō Ōishi, a nun belonging to the Shingon Buddhist school, had. After experiencing many difficulties in the earlier part of her life, she became a Buddhist. I want to discuss one episode in which she moved from one view of the self to another view of the self. [86]

## Rev. Junkyō Ōishi (1890–1965)

Rev. Ōishi's childhood dream was to become a professional Japanese dancer. Thus, when she was seventeen, she went to live in the house of a dance teacher in Kyoto. She was given the name Tsumakichi as a novice dancer. One night, a tragedy happened. The dance teacher's wife ran away with her boyfriend. On being informed of this, the dance teacher turned into a madman. He took out a sharp samurai sword and started to slash everybody he encountered. First, he chopped off the head, arms, and legs of his wife's mother. Then, he did the same to his wife's brother and sister. Then he attacked the three dance students who were in the house at the time. Tsumakichi was one of them.

When the bloody cutting and slashing were over, people found five dead bodies that were completely mutilated. In a pool of blood, they also found the barely moving body of a girl whose two arms were cut off from her shoulders. When a doctor examined her, he said that she would not live. But miraculously she did survive. This girl was Tsumakichi.

Having lost her arms, Tsumakichi had to give up her desire to become a dancer. Her life after that was not easy. She joined a circus and earned her living showing her armless body. She was one of the main attractions of the circus because she was known as the sole survivor of the famous "Slaughtering Incident in Kyoto."

## A Dance Recital

Then, one day when Tsumakichi was in her mid-twenties, some people offered her an opportunity to participate in a Japanese dance project. She was supposed to play the leading role in the dance called the Sambasō, one of the most famous Japanese dances that all Japanese dancers dream of dancing. How could she, an armless person, play the leading role in the dance? They planned it this way. Her two arms were to be played by two famous puppeteers wearing dark robes to hide their bodies. With one exposing his right arm and the other exposing his left arm, these two puppeteers would stand behind Tsumakichi and their arms were to accompany her dancing.

Tsumakichi was excited about this dance project, because it was her lifelong dream to dance the Sambasō. She and the two puppeteers practiced and practiced. But as the day of their performance got closer, they were frustrated because there wasn't coordination between Tsumakichi and the two puppeteers. Her body appeared to belong to one person and her arms to another. Tsumakichi got quite worried about the opening day.

A few days before the opening day, Tsumakichi had a hard time sleeping because she was anxious about the dance recital. Then all of a sudden she heard a voice telling her, "How conceited you are! How egoistic you are! You have been thinking that you are the lead dancer and those two arms should follow you. You have been so frustrated because those two arms do not follow your performance. But, don't you think that is a conceited idea? Those two puppeteers are professional artists, accomplished artists. They can handle a puppet, a lifeless doll, as if it were alive. They have no problem in handling you, a living being. Your ego is standing in the way. You are nothing but an amateur dancer. Why do you have to strain yourself to lead the dance? Why don't you become a puppet and let them guide you? Why don't you let the two arms guide you and just follow them?"

After she had this realization, there was perfect coordination between the two puppeteers and her. Their recital was a great success.

## Conclusion

Initially Tsumakichi saw her self as an independent and autonomous entity. She was thinking of her dancing only in terms of her own individual action. But when she had this realization, she understood that she was part of one organic whole, one organic interdependent movement. Now she started to see her self as a participant in an interdependent movement. Initially, because of her self-centeredness, her movement had an antagonistic relationship with the movements of the puppeteers. And she was so frustrated. But when she realized that she was part of an interdependent movement and submitted herself to the movement, she ceased to feel frustrated. There was perfect coordination between her and the two puppeteers.

This episode shows us the transition from the view of the self as something independent and autonomous to the view of the self as part of an organic whole. Here I can see the same type of spiritual experience that our teachers, such as Shakyamuni and Shinran, had.

# 19

# The Tip of the Iceberg

## Introduction

It is important to know the limits of human knowledge. Although we like to think our knowledge is extensive, it is very limited and there is so much we do not know. We are, as it were, seeing the tip of an iceberg; so much is hidden from our sight.[87]

In one of his essays, Dr. Kitarō Nishida talks about the inconceivable reality that exists behind our existence:

> On one dark winter day when the wind was blowing violently outside, people were talking in a room. Then, a bird entered the room through one window and flew out of it through another window. Where did the bird come from and where did it go? The people in the room agreed that human life was exactly like that.[88]

Dr. Nishida says that just as the people could not know where the bird came from and where it went, we human beings cannot know where we came from and where we are going. We can say the same thing about the law of causation—the basic teaching of Shakyamuni Buddha. The law of causation is often called "the inconceivable law of causation (*fukashigi-innen*)." The adjective "inconceivable" is added because there are limitless causes and conditions behind all existing things. We, however, can see only a small part of them. For example, although we usually know the names of our parents and grandparents, very few of us know the names of our great-grandparents or other earlier ancestors.

## Two Unforgettable Encounters

Let me here talk about a couple of experiences that taught me that I was seeing only a fragment of the limitless reality that exists behind all existing things.

About thirty years ago, not long after I came to this country from Japan, I lived in the Buddhist Temple of Chicago. The temple is located in an area known as Uptown. There were some halfway houses in that area. Near the Buddhist temple there was a street called Broadway, where I often saw people with mental problems.

Once I saw a middle-aged woman with a mental problem. Whenever she saw a bus on Broadway, she got angry with it and yelled all kinds of four letter words toward the bus. Since I had recently come from Japan and Japanese English teachers had never taught me English swear words, I did not understand what she was saying. But I could tell that she was saying something very nasty. Not only did she orally attack the bus, she also banged the side of the bus with her purse. When I saw her for the first time, I was really surprised by her behavior. Afterward, whenever I saw her doing these things, I had a feeling of contempt toward her.

But some time later, a friend told me that there were deep reasons for her strange behavior. I learned that she was so upset with buses because several years earlier her son had been run over and killed by a bus. She became insane because of her son's death. When I heard the tragic story, my contempt toward her turned into compassion. Until my friend told me about it, I could in no way have known that there was such a background there. I realized that I was seeing only the tip of an iceberg—a surface manifestation of the person.

Another incident took place in Madison, Wisconsin, when I was studying at the university there. The university campus was sandwiched between two lakes. I used to go out for a walk along one of the lakes. Every time I went to the lake, I saw a middle-aged man standing on the shore. He kept standing there for hours and hours. He did not move at all. He was obviously a mental patient. He looked at one spot in the lake with his mouth open. He looked not only weird but also comical. Thus, every time I saw him, I made fun of him in my mind, thinking, "Look, the same old guy is standing there with his mouth open!"

Then one day I happened to meet a fisherman at the lake. The fisherman and I started to talk. The fisherman told me, "Did you notice that guy standing there all day long? He looks kind of dumb. But, you know, several years ago, the boat that was carrying his wife and children capsized in the middle of the lake and they all were drowned. He became insane after that. You know, he goes to the same place every day. He is looking at the spot where his wife and children perished."

When I listened to this story, I realized that I was seeing only the tip of an iceberg—the surface appearance of the man, and that I was not seeing the causation that existed behind the man.

I have talked about my encounters with two insane people. In each encounter I recognized the narrowness of my perspective. Unless I was informed of their backgrounds by someone, there was no way I could know about them. I just had a feeling of contempt or sarcasm toward them.

Although we like to think that our understanding is absolute, deep, and certain, it is actually relative, shallow, and uncertain. Our understanding cannot help being that way, because this world consists of limitless causation and our understanding is so limited. We are just interpreting a given situation on the basis of our limited experience.

### The Zen Concept of *Ka-hitsu* ("Why Necessarily So?")

The Zen master Dōgen talks about a concept called *Ka-hitsu* ("Why necessarily so?")[89] that teaches us how we should see all things in this world. The meaning of this concept is as follows. Because this world consists of limitless causes and conditions and our knowledge is so limited, whatever interpretation we come up with concerning things in this world must be challenged with the question: "Why [is your interpretation] necessarily so?" Although we like to think that our interpretations are absolute, there is nothing absolute about them. We could have totally different interpretations if we had different backgrounds.

Here, to further explain the truth of "Why [is your interpretation] necessarily so?" I would like to talk about the parable of the five blind men and an elephant.

> Once upon a time a king gathered five blind men about an elephant and asked them to tell him what an elephant was like. The first blind man felt a tusk and said an elephant was like a giant carrot; another happened to touch an ear and said it was like a big fan; another touched its trunk and said it was like a pestle; still another, who happened to feel its leg, said it was like a mortar; and another, who grasped its tail, said it was like a rope. None of them was able to tell the king the elephant's real form.

As far as these blind men are concerned, there are two ways of touching the elephant: the right way and the wrong way.

The right way of touching the elephant is this: if they know that they are touching only small parts of the animal and their definitions are partial, that is the right way of touching an elephant. If they know that there are many other parts that they have not touched and other blind men are touching them and are coming up with other valid definitions, that is the right way of touching the animal. If they know that what they are touching is "Why is it necessarily so?" that is the right way of touching the elephant.

The wrong way of touching the elephant is this: if they think that they are touching the entirety of the elephant, that is the wrong way of touching it. If they think that their understandings are the only right ones and that the other blind men are wrong, that is the wrong way. If they don't know that what they are touching is "Why is it necessarily so?" that is the wrong way.

If those blind men take the right way of touching the animal, then they will not fight among themselves. But if they take the wrong way, they cannot help fighting among themselves.

We human beings are all precisely like the blind men. Just as each one of them is touching only a fragment of the animal and cannot touch its entirety, we are grasping only a fragment of this world and cannot grasp its entirety.

The Zen master Dōgen said: "A fish goes and it looks like a fish…

A bird flies and it is like a bird."[90] He says that "looks like" or "is like" is the only thing we can say about our recognition of the things of this world. There is only appearance, phenomenal appearance. What we are perceiving here and now is all there is in this world. If we see a thing that looks like a fish, we call it a fish. Maybe it is not a fish. But if we think it is a fish, it is a fish. If we see a thing that looks like a bird, we call it a bird. Maybe it is not a bird. But if we think it is a bird, it is a bird. Thus, Dōgen said, "A fish goes and it looks like a fish. A bird flies and it is like a bird."

This way Buddhism teaches us that our cognition is very shallow; it does not have any solid and firm basis. Everything is impermanent and is moving and changing so fast. Our recognition is part of this quickly changing reality. Dōgen says we cannot have any absolutely firm basis for our understanding of things and people. This is a tremendously humble way of understanding the manner in which we exist.

## The Meaning of *Namu Amida Butsu*

These two insights—insight into the limits of our knowledge and insight into the limitless reality that exists behind our existence—are the two-fold content of the *shinjin* experience. They are also the contents of Amida's Name, *Namu Amida Butsu*. The meaning of the three words contained in Amida's Name is as follows. *Butsu* (Buddhahood) means awakening. The other two words—*Namu* (Bowing) and *Amida* (Limitlessness)—express the two-fold content of the awakening: when one experiences *Namu* (Bowing), i.e., when one gains insight into the limits of his knowledge, he simultaneously experiences *Amida* (Limitlessness), i.e., he gains insight into the limitless reality that exists behind his existence.

The Buddha whose Name is *Namu Amida Butsu* (Bowing Limitlessness Buddha) is humble and dynamic. Because he knows his ignorance (*Namu*), he is eager to learn from a limitless number of teachers. Such a humble and dynamic person cannot help influencing other people. His *Namu* (Bowing) makes others have *Namu* too. The person who is *Namu Amida Butsu* cannot help influencing others and making them become *Namu Amida Butsu* too.

Hōnen embodied *Namu Amida Butsu*. When Shinran met Hōnen, he was deeply shaken by Hōnen's spirit of *Namu Amida Butsu*. Thus, Shinran also became *Namu Amida Butsu*. That is why Shinran called himself "Foolish-Baldheaded One"[91] when he gained insight into limitlessness. Only the person who can know himself or herself as a foolish person can know limitlessness. When Shinran recognized the limits of his knowledge, he recognized the limitlessness and inconceivability of the world he lived in.

## Conclusion

I can see *Namu Amida Butsu* in the following story of Isaac Newton, the great scientist.

One day Newton was staying at a seaside town. When he was looking at the ocean, one of his admirers approached him and said, "Mr. Newton, you are a really great scientist. You must know so many things about this universe." To this, Newton answered, "No, I don't know anything at all. Although you admire my wisdom, I don't know anything at all." Then, Newton pointed his finger at a boy who was on the beach. "Please look at that boy on the beach. The boy is so happy because he has picked up a couple of seashells there. I am just like that boy; I have discovered only a couple of truths. But the world of undiscovered truth is lying there just like the ocean. I know only a few things. Although you call me a wise person, I am not wise at all."

Yes, we are seeing only a small part of this world. There is so much that is hidden from our sight. We can in no way say that our understanding is thorough or absolute. Teachers such as Shakyamuni and Shinran teach us that we must know the limits of our knowledge. Goethe, a famous German novelist, said:

> The finest achievement for a man of thought is to have fathomed what may be fathomed, and quietly to revere the unfathomable.[92]

# Endnotes

1 Junjirō Takakusu and Kaikyoku Watanabe, eds., *Taishō Shinshū Daizōkyō* (henceforth *Taishō*) (Tokyo: Daizō Shuppan-sha, 1924–34), vol. 83, p. 728c3–5. Cf. *Collected Works of Shinran*, vol. 1 (henceforth *CW1*) (Kyoto: Jōdo Shinshū Hongwanji-ha, 1997), p. 662.

2 For a discussion of *icchantika*, see Shūichi Maida, *The Evil Person: Essays on Shin Buddhism,* trans. Nobuo Haneda (Los Angeles: Higashi Honganji North American Translation Center, 1989), pp. 77–83.

3 Haya Akegarasu, *Akegarasu Haya Zenshū* [The Complete Works of Haya Akegarasu] (Ishikawa, Japan: Myōtatsu-ji, 1956–60), pt. 2, vol. 8, pp. 560–65. For an English translation of this essay, see *The Dharma Breeze* (newsletter of the Maida Center of Buddhism), v-2 (1999), pp. 5–8.

4 Manshi Kiyozawa, *Kiyozawa Manshi Zenshū* [The Complete Works of Manshi Kiyozawa] (Tokyo: Iwanami Shoten, 2002–3), vol. 6, pp. 125–26. For an English translation of this essay, see *The Dharma Breeze*, v-2 (1999), pp. 8–9.

5 *Taishō*, vol. 83, p. 629b22. Cf. "Essential" gate in *CW1*, p. 221.

6 *Taishō*, vol. 83, p. 600c7. Cf. *CW1*, p. 74.

7 For Rev. Soga's discussion of Shinran's view of Buddhist history, see *An Anthology of Modern Shin Buddhist Writings* (Kyoto: Shin Buddhist Comprehensive Research Institute, Ōtani University, 2001), pp. 59–80.

8 For Rev. Soga's discussion of Dharmakara as the *alaya-vijnana*, see Ryōjin Soga, *Soga Ryōjin Senshū* [The Selected Works of Ryōjin Soga] (Tokyo: Yayoi-shobō, 1972), pp. 106–42. See also *An Anthology of Modern Shin Buddhist Writings*, pp. 45–57.

9 For further information concerning Akegarasu's life, see Shūichi Maida, *Heard by Me*, trans. Nobuo Haneda (Berkeley, California, Frog Press, 1992).

10 Haya Akegarasu, *Shinran Shōnin no shinnen* [The Religious

Conviction of Shinran Shōnin] (Ishikawa: Kōsōsha, 1925), p. 17–18. Cf. Haya Akegarasu, "On the Recent Popularity of Shinran," trans. Nobuo Haneda, *The Dharma Breeze*, vi-1 (2000), pp. 6–9.

11 Ibid., p. 18.

12 See below, pp. 101 and 124.

13 See above, p. 13.

14 For example, Shinran talks about becoming the supreme Buddha (that Amida symbolizes) in his "Chapter on Naturalness (*Jinen-hōni-shō*)." See *CW1*, p. 428.

15 *Taishō*, vol. 83, p. 633a2. Cf. *CW1*, p. 241.

16 Besides "bowing," *namu* (Skt. *namas*) has other meanings such as "taking refuge in," "worshipping," and "revering."

17 *Taishō*, vol. 12, p. 267b5–7. Cf. Hisao Inagaki, *The Three Pure Land Sutras* (henceforth *Inagaki*), BDK English Tripitaka 12-II (Berkeley: Numata Center, 1995), p. 29.

18 *Taishō*, vol. 12, p.269b25. Cf. *Inagaki*, p. 40.

19 See Leo Pruden, trans., *The Essentials of the Eight Schools*, BDK English Tripitaka 107-I (Berkeley: Numata Center, 1995), pp. 64–65.

20 *Taishō*, vol. 83, p. 549c9–10. Cf. *CW1*, p. 38.

21 *Taishō*, vol. 83, p. 728b1–2. Cf. *CW1*, p. 664.

22 *Taishō*, vol. 83, p. 784a18–21. Cf. Ann Rogers and Minor Rogers, trans., *Rennyo Shōnin Ofumi: The Letters of Rennyo*, BDK English Tripitaka 106-I (Berkeley: Numata Center, 1996), p. 48.

23 *Taishō*, vol. 12, p. 277c26–p. 278a9. Cf. *Inagaki*, pp. 83–84.

24 *Taishō*, vol. 12, p. 267b5–10. Cf. *Inagaki*, pp. 29–30.

25 *Taishō*, vol. 12, p. 606c23–25. Cf. *CW1*, pp. 108–9.

26 For Yasuda's view of the Pure Land, see Rijin Yasuda, *Yasuda Rijin Kōgi-shū* [A Collection of Lectures by Rijin Yasuda] (Tokyo: Yayoi-shobō, 1998), vol. 4.

27 For Yasuda's view of the Sangha as the Pure Land, see Rijin Yasuda, *Yasuda Rijin Kōgi-shū*, vol. 5, p. 125. *See also* "Sangha," *The Dharma Breeze*, vi-2 (2000), pp. 6–7.

28 *Taishō*, vol. 37, p. 273a17–18. Cf. *CW1*, p. 90.

29 *Taishō*, vol. 37, p. 273a12–13. Cf. *CW1*, p. 90.

30 In Shinran's teaching this stage is synonymous with *shinjin*, "birth in the Pure Land," and "the rightly determined stage." One who attains this stage will unfailingly attain Buddhahood. See *Taishō*, vol. 83, p. 694c25–p. 695a3. Cf. *CW1*, p. 476.

31 See above, pp. 9–10 and endnote 6.

32 Cf. *Inagaki*, pp. 91–118.

33 *Taishō*, vol. 12, p. 341b16–18. Cf. *Inagaki*, p. 95.

34 See above, pp. 11–12.

35 For a discussion of the visitation (*kuyō*) practice, see above, pp. 26–27.

36 *Taishō*, vol. 12, p. 272c17–p. 273b18. Cf. *Inagaki*, pp. 56–60.

37 For an English translation of the full title of Shinran's main work, see below, p. 90.

38 See below, pp. 108–10.

39 Shinran quotes this sentence in his "Verses of True Entrusting (*Shōshin-ge*)," *Taishō*, vol. 83, p. 600b17. Cf. *CW1*, p. 72.

40 For a discussion of self-love, see below, pp. 128–29.

41 *Taishō*, vol. 83, p. 657b1–2. Cf. *CW1*, p. 336, verse no. 48.

42 See above, p. 28.

43 *Taishō*, vol. 83, p. 660b1–3. Cf. *CW1*, p. 364, verse no. 13.

44 The parable of "Priceless Jewel" is found in the Lotus Sutra, *Taishō*, vol. 9, p. 29b. Cf. Tsugunari Kubo and Akira Yuyama, trans., *The Lotus Sutra*, BDK English Tripitaka 13-I (Berkeley: Numata Center, 1993), p. 161.

45 Cf. Charles Luk, trans., *The Shurangama Sutra* (London: Rider & Company, 1966), pp. 97–100.

46 For Mrs. Nakamura's life, see Hisako Nakamura, *The Hands and Feet of the Heart*, ed. Bunyū Fujimura (Los Angeles: The Nembutsu Press, 1991).

47 Shūichi Maida, *Maida Shūichi Zenshū* [The Complete Works of Shūichi Maida] (Nagano, Japan: Maida Shūichi Zenshū Kankōkai, 1969–71), vol. 1, pp. 341–42.

48 For an essay on this topic, see Shūichi Maida, "The Unique Feature of Buddhism," trans. Nobuo Haneda, *The Dharma Breeze*, ii (1996), pp. 3–4.

49  *Taishō*, vol. 83, p. 589a21. Cf. *CW1*, p. 4.

50  For Yasuda's view of tradition, see Rijin Yasuda, "Tradition," trans. Nobuo Haneda, *The Dharma Breeze*, vii-1 (2001), pp. 10–11.

51  Shūichi Maida, *Maida Shūichi Zenshū* [The Complete Works of Shūichi Maida], vol. 2, p. 228–29. Cf. Shūichi Maida, *Heard by Me*, pp. 134–35.

52  *Bashō Zenshū* [The Complete Works of Bashō], ed. Keion Nunami and Taseki Niekawa (Tokyo: Iwanami Shoten, 1928), p. 489.

53  *Taishō*, vol. 83, p. 267b29–c2. Cf. *Inagaki*, p. 31.

54  In the *Kyōgyōshinshō* Shinran has 376 quotes from 62 texts.

55  These words are mentioned in the first *kōan* of the *Mumonkan* [Gateless Gate], a collection of *kōan*s. Cf. Zenkei Shibayama, *Zen Comments on the "Mumonkan,"* trans. Sumiko Kudō (New York and Scarborough, Ontario: The New American Library, 1975), p. 20.

56  Cf. Dōgen, *A Primer of Sōtō Zen*, trans. Reihō Masunaga (Honolulu: The University Press of Hawaii, 1971), p. 49.

57  Cf. *CW1*, p. 290.

58  Cf. *CW1,* p. 474.

59  *Taishō*, vol. 83, p. 642c20. Cf. *CW1*, p. 290.

60  See below, p. 124.

61  For a discussion of the Shin view of these practices, see below, pp. 107–108

62  Cf. *CW1*, pp. 78, 206.

63  For Shinran's verse that talks about a *shinjin* person's attainment of *parinirvana* at the last moment of his life, see below, p. 109.

64  Shinran quotes this parable in his *Kyōgyōshinshō*. Cf. *CW1*, pp. 89–91.

65  *Taishō*, vol. 83, p. 698c12–15. Cf. *CW1*, p. 488.

66  *Taishō*, vol. 83, p. 653b17. Cf. *CW1*, p. 616.

67  *Taishō*, vol. 83, p. 655a18–19. Cf. *CW1*, p. 629.

68  *Taishō*, vol. 83, p. 665b29–c5, also p. 609b16–19. Cf. *CW1*, pp. 123, 405.

69  These three wonderful spiritual qualities are included in the ten wonderful spiritual qualities of the *shinjin* person. Concerning these ten

qualities, see *Taishō*, vol. 83, p. 607b21–26 or *CW1*, p. 112.

70  For a discussion of this topic, see Haya Akegarasu, "From the *Tannishō* to the *Larger Sutra*," trans. Nobuo Haneda, and Shūichi Maida, "Appendix to My Article, 'From the *Tannishō* to the *Larger Sutra*'," trans. Nobuo Haneda, *The Dharma Breeze*, v-1 (1999).

71  *Taishō*, vol. 82, p. 23c19–23. Cf. Dōgen, *Master Dōgen's Shōbōgenzō*, trans. Gudō Nishijima and Chōdō Cross (London: Windbell Publications, 1998), vol. 1, p. 34.

72  *Taishō*, vol. 82, p. 240a26–27. Cf. Dōgen, *Master Dōgen's Shōbōgenzō*, vol. 3, p. 266.

73  Shinran quotes the entire story of Ajatasatru in his *Kyōgyōshinshō*. See *CW1*, pp. 125–43.

74  *Taishō*, vol. 83, p. 728b8–22. Cf. *CW1*, p. 662.

75  Haya Akegarasu, *Akegarasu Haya Zenshū*, pt. 2, vol. 2, p. 147. Cf. Shūichi Maida, *Heard by Me*, p. 6.

76  Cf. Max Muller, ed., *Sacred Books of the East* (London: Oxford University Press, 1924), vol. 10, p. 156.

77  *Taishō*, vol. 12, p. 1112b18.

78  *Taishō*, vol. 83, p. 629c17. Cf. *CW1*, p. 222.

79  For information concerning this pen name, see Manshi Kiyozawa, *December Fan: The Buddhist Essays of Manshi Kiyozawa*, trans. Nobuo Haneda (Kyoto: Higashi Honganji, 1984), p. 85.

80  Cf. Shūichi Maida, *Heard by Me*, p. 46.

81  *Lamentations* 3: 29. King James Version has "He putteth his mouth in the dust; if so be there may be hope." *The New English Bible* (New York: Oxford University Press, 1961, 1970) has "let him lay his face in the dust, and there may yet be hope."

82  *Taishō*, vol. 83, p. 728c16–17. Cf. *CW1*, p. 663. For a discussion of the concept of the evil person, see Shūichi Maida, *The Evil Person: Essays on Shin Buddhism*, trans. Nobuo Haneda (Los Angeles: Higashi Honganji North American Translation Center, 1989).

83  *Taishō*, vol. 83, p. 707c14–15. Cf. *CW1*, p. 459.

84  Manshi Kiyozawa, *Kiyozawa Manshi Zenshū*, vol. 8, p. 363. Cf. Manshi Kiyozawa, *December Fan*, p. 25.

85  See above, p. 6.

86  For information concerning her life, see Junkyō Ōishi, *Mude no hōetsu* [The Dharma-joy of the Armless] (Tokyo: Shunjūsha, 1968).

87  For a discussion of the limits of human knowledge, see Shūichi Maida, "The Limits of Human Knowledge," trans. Nobuo Haneda, *The Dharma Breeze*, viii-2 (2002), pp. 4–6.

88  Kitarō Nishida, *Nishida Kitarō Zenshū* [The Complete Works of Kitarō Nishida] (Tokyo: Iwanami Shoten, 1965–66), vol. 12, p. 184.

89  *Taishō*, vol. 82, p. 24c29. Cf. Dōgen, *Master Dōgen's Shōbōgenzō*, vol. 1, p. 36.

90  *Taishō,* vol. 82, p. 120c27–28.  Cf. Dōgen, *Master Dōgen's Shōbōgenzō*, vol. 2, p. 106. For a discussion of these words of Dōgen, see Shūichi Maida, "The Limits of Human Knowledge," trans. Nobuo Haneda, *The Dharma Breeze*, viii-2 (2002), pp. 4–6.

91  See above, p. 90.

92  Goethe, Johann Wolfgang von, *Maxims and Reflections*, trans. Bailey Saunders (New York: Macmillan Company; London: Macmillan & Co., Ltd., 1906), p. 200, no. 577.

# Selected Bibliography

## Works in Japanese and Classical Chinese

Akegarasu, Haya. *Akegarasu Haya Zenshū* [The Complete Works of Haya Akegarasu]. 24 vols. Ishikawa, Japan: Myōtatsu–ji, 1956–60.

Kiyozawa, Manshi. *Kiyozawa Manshi Zenshū* [The Complete Works of Manshi Kiyozawa]. Edited by Ōtani University. 9 vols. Tokyo: Iwanami Shoten, 2002–3.

Maida, Shūichi. *Maida Shūichi Zenshū* [The Complete Works of Shūichi Maida]. 13 vols. Nagano, Japan: Maida Shūichi Zenshū Kankōkai, 1969–71.

Nakamura, Hisako. *Kokoro no teashi* [The Hands and Feet of the Heart]. Tokyo: Shunjūsha, 1973.

Ōishi, Junkyō. *Mude no hōetsu* [The Dharma-joy of the Armless]. Tokyo: Shunjūsha, 1968.

Soga, Ryōjin. *Soga Ryōjin Senshū* [The Selected Works of Ryōjin Soga]. Edited by Soga Ryōjin Senshū Kankōkai. 12 vols. Tokyo: Yayoi-shobō, 1971.

*Taishō Shinshū Daizōkyō* [Taishō Tripitaka]. Edited by Junjirō Takakusu and Kaikyoku Watanabe. 100 vols. Tokyo: Daizō Shuppan-sha, 1924–34.

Yasuda, Rijin. *Yasuda Rijin Senshū* [The Selected Works of Rijin Yasuda]. Edited by Yasuda Rijin Senshū Hensan Iinkai. 15 vols. Kyoto: Bun'eidō.

## Works in English

Akegarasu, Haya. *Shout of Buddha*. Translated by Gyōkō Saitō and Joan Sweany. Chicago: Orchid Press, 1977.

*An Anthology of Modern Shin Buddhist Writings*. Edited by Ōtani University. Kyoto: Shin Buddhist Comprehensive Research Institute, Ōtani University, 2001.

*Collected Works of Shinran.* 2 vols. Kyoto: Jōdo Shinshū Hongwanjiha, 1997.

Dōgen. *Master Dōgen's Shōbōgenzō.* Translated by Gudō Nishijima and Chōdō Cross. 4 vols. London: Windbell Publications, 1998.

Gomez, Luis O., trans. *The Land of Bliss: The Paradise of the Buddha of Measureless Light.* Honolulu: University of Hawaii Press and Kyoto: Higashi Honganji Shinshū Ōtani-ha, 1996.

Inagaki, Hisao, trans. *The Three Pure Land Sutras.* BDK English Tripitaka 12-II. Berkeley: Numata Center, 1995.

Kiyozawa, Manshi. *December Fan: The Buddhist Essays of Manshi Kiyozawa.* Translated by Nobuo Haneda. Kyoto: Higashi Honganji, 1984.

Maida, Shūichi. *The Evil Person: Essays on Shin Buddhism.* Translated by Nobuo Haneda. Los Angeles: Higashi Honganji North American Translation Center, 1989.

Maida, Shūichi. *Heard by Me: Essays on My Buddhist Teacher.* Translated by Nobuo Haneda. Berkeley, California: Frog Press, 1992.

Nakamura, Hisako. *The Hands and Feet of the Heart.* Edited by Bunyū Fujimura. Los Angeles: The Nembutsu Press, 1991.

# Index